Crash Course in Library Supervision

Recent Titles in
Libraries Unlimited's Crash Course Series

Crash Course in Library Supervision

Meeting the Key Players

Dennis C. Tucker and Shelley Elizabeth Mosley

Crash Course

LIBRARIES
UNLIMITED
A Member of the Greenwood Publishing Group

Westport, Connecticut • London

Library of Congress Cataloging-in-Publication Data

Tucker, Dennis C.
    Crash course in library supervision : meeting the key players /
Dennis C. Tucker and Shelley Elizabeth Mosley.
        p. cm. — (Crash course)
    Includes bibliographical references and index.
    ISBN-13: 978–1–59158–564–0 (alk. paper)
    1. Library personnel management—Handbooks, manuals, etc.
2. Library administration—Handbooks, manuals, etc.   3. Supervision
of employees—Handbooks, manuals, etc. I. Mosley, Shelley, 1950–
II. Title.
    Z682.T83 2008
    023—dc22   2007030131

British Library Cataloguing in Publication Data is available.

Library of Congress Catalog Card Number: 2007030131
ISBN: 978–1–59158–564–0

First published in 2008

Libraries Unlimited, 88 Post Road West, Westport, CT 06881
A Member of the Greenwood Publishing Group, Inc.
www.lu.com

Printed in the United States of America

The paper used in this book complies with the
Permanent Paper Standard issued by the National
Information Standards Organization (Z39.48–1984).

10 9 8 7 6 5 4 3 2 1

CONTENTS

ACKNOWLEDGMENTS

Many, many thanks to the following people for their valuable contributions to this project:

- Jessica and David Mosley for their much-appreciated technical support and indispensable advice.
- Andrew and Jennifer Mosley for their unfailing encouragement in this project as well as others.
- Jennie and Vicki Burrell for their ready willingness to assist, no matter what the project.
- Sandra Lagesse and Marion Ekholm, critique partners par excellence, for their insightful comments and observations.
- Lupe Sierra, deputy human resources director, Glendale, Arizona, for her cooperation and clarification.
- H. Marie Predmore, of the Indiana Cooperative Library Services Authority, for applying her excellent editing skills to not only this but also many other manuscripts over the years.
- Faye Terry and Edythe S. Huffman, from the Indiana State Library, for contributing what they have learned during their many years working with public libraries of all sizes throughout that state.

CHAPTER 1

Settling In: Getting to Know You

> No man is an Island, entire of itself; every man is a piece of the Continent, a part of the main.
>
> —John Donne, 1572–1631, Meditation XVII

INTRODUCING YOURSELF

Congratulations! You have a new job! You feel positively wonderful about being the successful candidate for this position, and rightfully so. The competition for jobs is fierce.

How did you get to be a library supervisor, manager, or director? Was it an in-house promotion? Did you transfer from another library in the same area? Did you hear about the position in a national job hotline and move from another state to take it?

It doesn't matter how you got this position. The bottom line is, you have it. You're ready to start this next step in your career. So now what do you do?

It's only natural to be overwhelmed and feel as though you need to do everything at once, but these first few days are precious and something you can never get back. This is the time when you meet the people who can help make your tenure in the library a success. You begin building the foundation of your connections with the staff, the library board, the Friends of the Library, government officials, and the public. These relationships are vital if you want to succeed.

Whether you were an in-house or outside candidate makes a difference in the first meeting with the staff. Both scenarios are outlined below. Some of this advice may sound elemental and obvious, but the number of library supervisors, managers, and directors who get off on the wrong foot with their staff is amazing.

FIRST IMPRESSIONS, LASTING IMPRESSIONS

Michelle Sterling, the founder of Global Image Group and an expert on image, impression, and impact, has written:

> Within the first three seconds of a new encounter, you are evaluated...even if it is just a glance. People appraise your visual and behavioral appearance from head to toe. They observe your demeanor, mannerisms, and body language and even assess your grooming and accessories—watch, handbag, briefcase. Within only three seconds, you make an indelible impression....Once the first impression is made, it is virtually irreversible.[1]

Your demeanor at your first meetings is very important. Smile. Greet everyone personally. You're going to make mistakes as a new director, but friendly people tend to be forgiven faster than those who are perceived to be aloof or unfriendly.

You're probably going to be anxious about the initial meetings with everyone, but try not to display your nervous habits, such as biting your fingernails or tapping your fingers on the table. Mannerisms are those little things that can drive people crazy. To be forewarned is to be forearmed. For example, if you're a pen clicker, don't carry your pen with you.

Body language is something people read almost subconsciously, so you want yours to be friendly. Smile. Make eye contact. Lean slightly forward when someone's talking to you. This indicates interest. Don't cross your arms over your chest. That's a sign of shutting yourself off from the person who's talking to you. By the way, if you never smile and don't much like to be around people, you have no business supervising anyone!

Overused buzzwords and jargon don't belong in your initial meetings. (In fact, they probably don't belong in any meeting!) "Synergy," "empowerment," "moving the cheese," "shifting paradigms," and other such words and phrases coming from a newcomer tend to make people bored, suspicious...or giggly. If you must use such a term, be sure to explain it.

The power of a name is not to be underestimated. Be prepared! Get a list of staff and board members. Try to familiarize yourself with the names before your first day of work. That way, you'll associate faces with names faster when you meet them. We know firsthand that it works, because we used to have a job that involved meeting a new group of people every week. By getting a list of names and studying it ahead of time, we were once able to greet by first and last name a group of 33 people within two days. Bring name tags with you to your first meetings so you can call people by name. Don't be shy about asking people to write their name in large letters! A city manager we know made it a practice to introduce himself to staff at all levels, look them in the eye, smile, and repeat their names after they had said them. From then on, he would call that person by name. This made everyone from custodians to upper management feel like a valued part of the team. On the other end of the spectrum, we know a technical services clerk who announced at a meeting that the library director rarely came to their department, and when she did, she didn't speak to anyone except the supervisor. The clerk said she felt "invisible" and doubted that the director even knew her name.

MEETING THE STAFF

If you're an outside candidate, or a person who wasn't part of the organization when you got your position, you can bet that the staff have searched the Internet and called their friends and colleagues to find out everything they can about you. (What you post on the Web, including on social Web sites, *can* come back to haunt you!)

Hopefully by now, someone has taken you around the library and introduced you to everyone. If not, you might ask someone to do so. Even if they have, you still need to have a get-acquainted meeting and one-on-one sessions with the staff. (One-on-one meetings are explained in the next chapter.) If no one has introduced you to the staff, you're more of an unknown element. Either way, you should have your get-acquainted meeting as soon as possible. It's important to remember that these meetings do not take the place of your one-on-one meetings. Both types are highly desirable.

THE GET-ACQUAINTED MEETING

You should have get-acquainted meetings with several groups: the staff, the library board, and the Friends of the Library. The basic structure of these meetings is similar, but some of the information you need to share may vary from group to group.

What does the staff want to know about you if you're an outside candidate? Well, what have you wanted to know about your new bosses when you were in a similar situation? Their experience? Their management style? A little bit about who they are? Your new staff is just as curious as you'd be.

What does the staff want to know about you if you're an in-house candidate? Sometimes starting off on the right foot is harder for the successful in-house candidate than for someone from the outside. You need to be especially sensitive to the other staff members who unsuccessfully applied for the job. Be prepared to deal with some bad or envious feelings. Some of them will want to know why you got this job and they didn't (something you can't and *shouldn't* address). Refer them to the human resources or personnel department instead). Some will want to know why you wanted this job in the first place. You might find it helpful to mention that the selection process is behind you now and that it is your desire to move forward as a team in a supportive and cooperative atmosphere. The staff needs enough information to begin to connect with you in your new role. You will find that once you become director, old friendships and relationships change. The staff wants to know how you will fulfill your *new* role.

What does the library board want to know about you? They want reassurance that you have the experience to do the job. They want to know if you're likeable and easy to work with. They want to know if you'll solicit their advice and listen to what they have to say.

What do the Friends of the Library want to know about you? They, too, want to know if you're likeable and easy to work with. They want to know if you have the experience to do the job. They want to know if you'll solicit their advice and listen to their suggestions.

Here is the basic structure for the get-acquainted meeting:

- Smile and greet people individually as they come in to the room. Pay attention to the culture of your organization, even when it comes to something as simple as what you want people to call you. In one organization, where everyone from the meter readers to the mayor was called by his or her first name, a new employee insisted on being referred to as "Mr. Smith" and spent an inordinate amount of time correcting anyone who didn't comply. His aloof actions alienated staff, and he became a textbook example that behavior trumps labels when it comes to connecting with people.

- Include everyone in the meeting. Custodians, secretarial staff, volunteers, and pages are often overlooked. Yet, these people are the backbone of your organization. Their support is vital.
- If, because of staff members' conflicting schedules, you need to hold more than one meeting, do it.
- Have food! Serve donuts or cookies and something to drink. Remember the old adage "The way to a man's heart is through his stomach"? Guess what: The way to most people's hearts is through their stomachs. One library director who has a very good relationship with her board buys a couple of fresh-baked pies before each meeting. The members of the board look forward to this treat and even offer suggestions for types of pies for the next meeting.
- Be sure to comment on how glad you are to be at this library and part of their team. Don't forget to tell them that you look forward to working with them. Remind them that you're relying on them to teach you about the library.
- The staff need some information so they can begin to connect with you:

  - Tell them a little bit about yourself, such as where you went to school, your marital status, whether you have kids, and if you have any hobbies or special interests. What would you want to know about a new boss if you were in their shoes?
  - Discuss why you want to work in this particular library.
  - Talk about your library experience.
  - Explain your management style. Don't leave 'em guessing!

    - Do you have an open-door philosophy?
    - Are you a hands-on supervisor?
    - Are you (Heaven help everyone) a micromanager? Most people would like to be reassured that you're not!

  - Don't blow your horn too loudly! That you played first violin in your high school orchestra, graduated summa cum laude, and have or been in every edition of *Who's Who* since 1985 isn't relevant, and telling your staff or board these things just makes you sound like a brag-gart. Remember, the purpose of this meeting is to make a good impression, not bore everyone to tears or make them take an instant dislike to you by proving that you're the director because you're so much better than they are.

- Open the floor for questions. Be honest in your answers. If you don't know something or prefer not to answer a particular question, be honest enough to say so candidly.
- Announce your upcoming one-on-one meetings.
- Give the people you're meeting with an idea of your vision for the library. If you're still forming your vision and don't have any firm ideas yet, tell them. If you'll be seeking their input—and you should be—let them know.

A GET-ACQUAINTED MEETING WITH THE PUBLIC

You might consider having an open house at the library so the public can meet you. This doesn't have the time-related urgency of your other meetings and can wait a little while if necessary. Sometimes the library board will want to host such a meeting for people to meet their new director. You should be spending some time at the public desks so you can meet your "regulars."

MEETING GOVERNMENT OFFICIALS

Whether you work for a town, city, county, or state library, government officials will be involved. These officials can include a mayor, town or city council members, a town or city manager, county supervisors, or even a governor. The members of this governing body will have the authority to increase your budget, decrease your budget, approve new hires, build a new facility, improve yours, or even close you down. In short, these are people who have a lot of power over your library.

You need to get to know your government officials, if for no other reason than it's easier for them to cut your budget if they have no idea who you are. Make it a point to set up an appointment to meet them, as well as their secretaries and assistants. Having a good relationship with the secretary can often cut through lots of red tape and save you a lot of time and phone tag!

MEETING THE LOCAL MEDIA (PUT YOURSELF IN THE PAPER!)

Find out if the library board or someone else traditionally issues a press release when there is a new director. If not, you can write it yourself. It's okay to blow your horn in a press release! *Now* you can let the public know that you've been in *Who's Who* or that you won the employee of the year award at McDonald's while you were still a teenager or used to sing in an award-winning barbershop quartet.

How do you write a press release? A press release has certain elements that need to be included:

- A contact person and phone number.
- The date you want the press release to go public. If you want it printed as soon as you can get it in the paper, write "For Immediate Release."
- Use an easy-to-read font, such as Courier or Times New Roman, in 12 point. Your press release should be double-spaced, on one side of the paper only, and as error free as possible. Add a picture if you have one. Don't expect to get it back.
- Some newspapers let you send information electronically. Ask about their policy first.

Use this initial contact to build your network with the media. You can follow it up with a phone call. Be sure to thank the editor for including your press release in the paper.

IN SUMMARY

Some people get so wrapped up in technobabble or the latest and greatest buzzwords that they tend to overlook the human side of things. Chances are, you've been a bundle of nerves during the hiring process for your new position. The people who are going to report to you are nervous, too, since you are the one who will be setting the tone of their workplace until you leave and someone else takes charge. Connect with your staff as soon as possible with group meetings followed by one-on-one meetings. Alleviate their concerns and answer their questions. Let your staff at all levels, as well as your volunteers, know from the get-go that you value them—and mean it. The relationships you form from the very first day are the key to your success.

NOTE

1. "First Impressions," http://entrepreneurs.about.com/cs/marketing/a/uc051603a.htm. Accessed April 2, 2007.

CHAPTER 2

Getting to Know the Staff: Listen and Learn

No man ever listened himself out of a job.
—President Calvin Coolidge (1872–1933)

Now that you're on board, you need to get to know the staff as quickly as possible. It's important to enlist them as allies. Remember that you are an unknown entity to the staff and that they are eager to find out who you are and how you work. Even if you're an insider hired for the position, relationships will immediately change, and staff members are likely wondering how you're going to function in your new role.

Of course, the way to get to know people is by talking with them. This can be done both formally and informally. In chapter 1, we talked about having a get-acquainted meeting with staff. In this chapter, we go beyond that and talk about meeting staff members individually, for your benefit and theirs. Don't lose sight of our chapter subtitle: "Listen and Learn."

ONE-ON-ONE MEETINGS

One of the first things we like to do after starting a new position is to have a one-on-one meeting with each staff member. If your library is small, it is easier to meet with everyone who works there. But if your library is too large to make this feasible (after all, you *do* have other things to do), at the very least meet with each direct report, that is, each person who reports directly to you and whom you are responsible for evaluating when it's evaluation time.

In conducting your one-on-one visits, don't overlook any department or area. You might consider visiting first those areas of the library with which you will be dealing most closely. That way, should a situation arise, you'll be prepared to deal with it.

JOB SHADOWING AND WORKING ALL THE DESKS

We like to use a technique called job shadowing, which basically means you follow each person around and observe what he or she does during the day. Tell the staff member not to be nervous; you're not there to critique or evaluate. Your purpose for this exercise is to learn how the library, and each position, functions. You also want to be prepared so that if this staff member comes to you in the future with a particular issue, you'll have some idea what he or she is talking about.

Of course, you don't really just chase people around. Tell the staff member to follow the usual daily routing as much as possible but to be prepared for interruptions and explanations if there's something you don't understand. Unless it's an area that's quite familiar to you, ask the staff member to explain each task as it's being performed. (This will also help you learn who would be a good trainer when a new staffer comes on board; if someone can explain it to you, he or she will likely be able to explain it to a new person in that position. Also, you may find someone who would be good at writing a procedure manual if one needs to be developed.)

Don't spring your visit on the staff person. Set it up well in advance. Try to find a time that won't have to be cancelled due to other commitments on the part of one or the other. Try to find a time when the staff person's routine will be as close to normal as possible. Try to find a time when the library will be quiet and free of interruptions to either of you.

How long should these visits be? It depends entirely on the situation and the individuals involved. Ideally, you'd have several days to get to know the person and get a good overview of everything that's involved in the job; some jobs can be extremely different from day to day. Realistically, however, that's probably not possible. But certainly, you want to spend enough time with each staff member to make the person feel that you really care and enough time to give you a good overview of the job. At a minimum, spend at least a couple of uninterrupted hours together. Hopefully, you can have more than one visit, because, as we have already noted, many jobs vary greatly from day to day. You definitely want to spend enough time with each person to make him or her feel important. Don't rush through the visit; it's better to cancel and reschedule than to leave the staff member feeling shorted.

Questions to Ask

You will want to ask some general get-acquainted questions such as these:

- "How long have you been at the library?"
- "What other positions have you held at the library before this position?" "How long were you in that position?" "What did you do in that position?"
- "What do you like best about working at the library? Why?"
- "What do you like least?"
- "What are the most difficult parts of your job? Why?"
- "Is there anything you need to make your job easier/better/ more efficient?"
- "What works about this position?"
- "What doesn't work? Why not?"
- "What needs to be different?"
- And, perhaps most important, "What can *I* do to improve your situation at work?"

Make sure your questions are open ones, not questions that can be answered quickly by a yes or no. Good open questions often start with the six magic words: who, what, when, where, why, how. Try to elicit answers that will give you the best sense of the person and the job. You want to try to produce dialogue, not just get a few perfunctory replies.

Always be sincere in your questions and your responses. Staff are likely to see right through superficiality, and it will not start you off on the path you want to follow.

You might want to throw in a couple of questions about the future, such as "Where do you see yourself in five years?" This will help you understand the staff member's goals and ambitions. It can help you determine whether you have someone who'd like to stay put for the long haul or that you may have a potential future department head on your hands.

Not only for legal reasons but because some people find them objectionable, you must be sure to avoid any questions of a personal nature, such as "Are you married?" or "How many children do you have?" If staff members volunteer the information, however, it's perfectly all right to ask follow-up questions. If they mention having children, it's fine to ask their names or other questions about them. And if they mention grandkids, you'd better ask about them! If you find yourself on a topic that makes you uncomfortable, the staff member may be as well, so it's best to avoid such an area. If you have a doubt about something, consult the library's legal counsel.

It's very important to let your staff know that you care about them as people. They are people first, workers second. But in this litigious day and age, we all must be very careful to avoid crossing that subtle line between being caring and being nosy. Pay full attention to your staff members and be sure to note whether they are eager to share their personal lives or are more private. You will find individuals of both types. Be interested but don't pry.

Be sure to focus most of your attention on the job itself. Don't hesitate to ask, "How do you do this?" or to request, "Show me how you do this." In many situations, a detailed overview of the position will be sufficient, unless you expect to have to perform the duties yourself sometime or to train someone to do them. Make sure you understand things thoroughly, but don't waste time on detail that you really don't need to know. Of course, in a small library, the director may work each desk and fill in at other jobs from time to time. In any case, you must learn enough about the job so that you can later evaluate whether the person is doing it well or not.

This is a good time to be careful of what *not* to say. Avoid the temptation to say, "At my old library, we did it this way." If the job is one you're familiar with (perhaps this visit is with your serials clerk and you spent many years as a serials clerk), be ready and willing to offer suggestions if the person is open to them. But this is not the time to "upset the applecart." Your real goal is to establish the highest level of trust possible so that later, if necessary, you and the staff member can have an open dialogue and institute change when and where needed. Barging in too quickly and imposing changes *now* will destroy any possibility of trust and, perhaps, even pit the staff member against you.

Bear in mind that you want to build up the trust level so that later, at evaluation time, the staff person understands that you're evaluating job performance, not personal likes and dislikes. Right now *you* are the learner, not the teacher.

MBWA: MANAGING BY WALKING AROUND

You may have heard people talk (i.e., complain) about managers in a bottle or managers who are out of touch. It's unfortunate that there are such managers, but it's a reality. Don't let yourself become one of them. It's now, at the beginning of your tenure, that you need to establish your work habits. It's also right now, at the beginning of your tenure, that you're probably bogged down, trying to learn everything you need to know for the new job. You may be up to your ears in paperwork, either because there's so much of it or because it takes too long, since you haven't yet learned the routine. You're trying to get acquainted with people, particularly the board and those outside the library. It's easy to overlook what's going on internally because of everything that's happening externally. Don't let it happen to you!

Start by getting up out of your chair, out of your office, and walking around the library. Stop and greet people by name! Ask how they're doing and how things are going. But expect an answer. If it initiates dialogue, so much the better.

Don't be like one manager we knew: If it was Friday, we knew that it was the manager's day for MBWA. He'd poke his head in the door, say, "How's it going?" and be gone before we had a chance to reply. Or he'd make a comment that elicited no response, like, "I got a phone call from so-and-so this week. Glad to hear everything's going so well over here." Things may *not* have been going so well from our perspective, but so-and-so told him that they were, so he assumed the opinion was universal. Of course, staff always knew that they needed to look busy on Friday because the boss would be around! And after he'd done his walk-through, he wouldn't be back.

MBWA is not to be confused with micromanaging, where you hover in one place for long periods at a time and watch every little thing the employee does until his or her nerves are stretched to the breaking point.

MBWA, if used properly, is a valuable tool for many reasons. It provides you with a change of pace. It gives you the opportunity to get out of your office and see what's going on in the library. It gives you the opportunity to show staff that you care about them and what's going on in their departments. It gives you an opportunity to speak with people and find out what's going on that's important to them. Use it frequently.

As you are walking around, be sure to greet people by name. This is especially true if you are a new director; people appreciate knowing that you have learned who they are, that they are identifiable individuals, not just someone doing a job. As you stop to talk with people, ask open-ended questions. And take time to listen to their answers. If someone says something that might be important, it wouldn't hurt to take notes; this is a way of saying to people, "I care. This is important to me."

STAFF MEETINGS

Once you have gotten to know the staff, you must provide ample opportunity for them to participate in the running of the library. Regular staff meetings are vital to a smooth-functioning operation.

The frequency of the meetings depends on the situation in the library, but monthly or every six weeks seems to be a good time frame for most libraries. Do whatever works for your situation. It may be necessary in some cases to have duplicate meetings to allow those with conflicting schedules to participate. Some larger libraries have a meeting for the librarians and another for support staff—not to discriminate, but because the two groups often have different types of issues to discuss.

The primary purpose of a staff meeting is communication. Remember the prefix "com-," meaning "with." Communication is two way, you with the staff and the staff with you. To be a successful director, you must ensure that communication is bidirectional.

One of the tenets of management is that if the official channels of communication are empty, the unofficial channels will quickly fill up. If you keep staff in the dark, there will be lots of "water-cooler" talk. The grapevine will quickly fill with speculation and rumor. The end result will be an unhealthy work atmosphere, perhaps filled with suspicion and misgiving.

Use staff meetings to provide information about what the staff wants to know. At the end of the official agenda, give staff members the opportunity to raise questions or problems. Answer them in the most straightforward manner possible. They will appreciate your frankness and honesty. If you don't know or aren't prepared to give a response yet, say so in a straightforward manner.

We have just a few more pointers on staff meetings. Have a purpose for each meeting; know what you want to accomplish and be able to determine (during the meeting) when you have accomplished it. Have a specific agenda and stick to it, allowing, of course, the opportunity at specific points for others to bring up new items. It's a good idea to have a printed agenda and to distribute it well before the meeting. (Before preparing the agenda, issue a call for items to the staff to make sure that items of interest to them are on the agenda.) Keep the meetings lively and brief. If you expect a dull meeting, bring food! Don't meet if you don't need to. There's nothing wrong with cancelling or postponing a meeting if you have nothing important to say and no one has requested that urgent items be addressed.

STANDING APPOINTMENTS

In addition to your regular meetings with staff as a group, individual one-on-one meetings are vital, particularly with your direct reports, department heads, or area leaders. A great technique is to set a standing appointment with each one. We suggest meeting monthly. For example, you might set an appointment to meet with the head of the public services department at 10:00 A.M. on the third Thursday of each month. Since you will likely be seeing this person at the staff meeting each month, you might want to stagger the standing appointment so that it hits halfway between staff meetings.

There are several advantages to working from a standing appointment:

1. It provides a regular time for you to meet with your direct reports; things won't fall "between the cracks" or get put off too long due to a lack of a time you can meet.

2. If there are small items that can wait, either of you can simply jot a note to yourself, stick it in a file, and bring up the note during the appointment. That way, you don't have to go chasing each other or play phone tag over items that can wait.

3. This is a time the two of you can work in private and without interruption. This is especially important if you need to discuss personnel matters.

4. If you have weighty matters to discuss, as you often might with one of your direct reports, you already have a preestablished time in which to do so.

5. A regular standing appointment is a way for you, the director, to say to your staff member through your actions, "You

and your job are important enough for me to set aside some time exclusively for you."

Each of you should have a list of items you need to deal with at the meeting. We've found it helpful to let the direct report go first, then to bring up our topics later, if they haven't already come up.

Again, don't meet just for meeting's sake. Communicate with each other a day or two before the meeting and if neither of you has any items worth discussing, cancel!

IN SUMMARY

The library's staff is its most important asset. Staff members deserve, and need, as much time as you can possibly devote to them. As a new director, one of the most important things you can do is get to know the staff right away. There are various techniques for doing so, including an initial get-acquainted staff meeting and job shadowing.

Once you're on board as director, it is vital to keep communication channels open. Regular staff meetings are vital. Standing appointments with your direct reports can be another valuable tool. Keeping in touch with your staff will prevent miscommunication, misconceptions, and missteps on your road to being the best director you possibly can be.

CHAPTER 3

Managing Personnel: Tips to Make Your Life Easier

The Golden Rule: *Do to others as you would have them do to you.* (Luke 6:31, NIV)

The Platinum Rule: *Do unto others as they would have you do unto them.*

GETTING TO KNOW THE HUMAN RESOURCES OR PERSONNEL DIRECTOR

One of the first people you should make an acquaintance with is the human resources, or personnel, director. Unless you're in a large library, the personnel director will probably be someone outside the library who functions in this capacity for your umbrella organization (town, city, state, etc.). Set up an appointment, or better yet, take that person out to coffee. This takes care of interruptions that will invariably occur if you stay in either the library or the human resources department.

Before this meeting, read the employee handbook and personnel rules *thoroughly* and make note of any questions you have regarding them. The list of questions you prepare for your meeting with the human resources director might include the following:

- What are the most common errors new supervisors in this organization make?
- How can I go about avoiding these errors?
- How would you describe the organizational culture?
- Is there any training that I should attend?
- Do you have any training opportunities for my staff?

It's better to get clarification now than to interpret the rules on your own and make a mistake later. Every organization is just a little bit different, so don't assume that because your previous employer did things a certain way, the same holds true in your new job!

These questions would also make a good starting point for discussions with your supervisor, as well as the president of your library board.

GET A COPY OF YOUR ORGANIZATION'S HUMAN RESOURCES/PERSONNEL RULES—AND FOLLOW THEM!

Not only should you have a copy of the human resources/personnel rules in your office, there should be a set at each desk, a copy readily available to every staff member. Some organizations have their personnel rules online, which makes for easy access by all.

Personnel manuals may cover the following information:

- Affirmative Action guidelines
- Attendance and leave policies: bereavement leave, family leave, holidays, jury duty, leave of absence, maternity leave, military leave, personal leave, professional leave, sabbaticals, sick leave, vacations
- Benefits (including insurance coverage)
- Classification plan
- Collective bargaining
- Compensation
- Disciplinary actions
- Dual-employment policy
- Employee conduct

- Employee grievance procedure
- Employee performance evaluation system
- Leave payouts or separation pay
- Limited-duty assignments
- Out-of-class assignments
- Overtime pay
- Promotions and demotions
- Retirement plans
- Savings sharing program
- Selection process: internal candidates, external candidates
- Separations: resignations, retirements, workforce reductions/layoffs/ reductions in force (RIFs)/displacements, transfers
- Standby pay
- Training
- Travel
- Tuition waivers
- Veterans' preference
- Work schedules: alternative work schedules, telecommuting, meals and rest breaks
- Workplace harassment
- Workplace violence

As you can see, this is a lot of information to know, but as director, it is your responsibility to be familiar with these guidelines, rules, policies, and laws and to enforce them. Failure to do so can result in anything from the loss of your job to a lawsuit.

COMMUNICATE, COMMUNICATE, COMMUNICATE!

Communication breakdowns with your staff can cause more damage than you'll ever want to deal with. It's up to you as director to take steps that prevent this from happening in your library. For starters, be sure that you have an open-door policy. An open-door policy has two parts, one literal and one psychological. The first part is easy: Leave the door to your office open while you're at work. The second part is harder, and maybe even more important: Employees should feel free to talk to you at any time, unless you have a meeting in progress or are otherwise engaged.

If your library has shift changes—at the circulation or reference desk, for example—make sure there are debriefings at those shift changes. Those who are leaving need to pass along items of vital interest to those arriving. These debriefings can be as short as a minute or two, but the information may be immediately relevant. An example of this might be relaying information on a computer problem the previous shift was experiencing and telling how they overcame it, in case the problem re-occurs. An alternative, which offers the additional advantage of providing a written record, is to use something like a blog that is easily accessible to all staff members at that service point.

Weekly staff meetings, which we covered in more depth in chapter 2, are a good way to get information and updates from each department, but don't make them too long. In corporate America, some managers have been known to have everyone stand during meetings to limit the length of meetings. Some people suggest that meetings should never last more than 45 minutes, but don't make your meetings so brief that the staff isn't given a chance to voice opinions or offer suggestions. Post an agenda before your meeting and let staff add items they think should be covered.

If you have the staff and the time, a monthly, quarterly or bian-nual newsletter is a good way to augment communications. The caveat here is that creating a newsletter is quite time-consuming, so be sure you have the staff and resources to do it without burdening the rest of the employees. Many newsletters have died because of the difficulty of getting people to contribute news items. Produce a newsletter only if you find it useful. Determine what you want to accomplish, and don't waste time and energy unless the newsletter is meeting that need. To save resources, consider an online newsletter.

While we're on the subject of communication, make a point of keeping your supervisor in the loop; share the good, as well as the bad. Failing to keep your supervisor informed can damage, or end, even the most promising career.

ENCOURAGING TEAMWORK

Patrick Lencioni, president of management consulting firm the Table Group and author of several best-selling books, has identified five dysfunctions of a team: absence of trust, fear of conflict, lack of commitment, avoidance of accountability, and inattention to results.[1] Absence of trust makes people feel vulnerable, with the worst case being actual paranoia. Fear of conflict kills all hope of honest communication. Lack of commitment comes when people stop expressing themselves honestly and don't buy into policies or projects. Avoidance of account-ability comes when no one is called on poor performance. Inattention to results takes place when a team member's ego becomes too big and that person is so focused on individual accomplishments that the needs and accomplishments of the team as a whole go unnoticed.

You want a fully functional team, and any single one of these five dysfunctions can ruin that functionality. Your team needs to be able to trust you, feel confident to take risks and offer their opinions, know that you share their commitment, feel accountable for the library and its operations, and think about themselves as team members as well as individuals on career tracks.

A well-functioning team doesn't happen overnight. It is something that needs to be developed. Trust and appreciation are two of the key elements of teamwork.

The first step toward teamwork is treating all employees with respect. Don't treat them as members of a hierarchy. The page staff is just as important as the senior reference people to the operation of the library. Think not? Consider the consequences of even one cart of books being put away incorrectly. Everyone needs to feel like an important part of the organization.

Recognize staff both individually and as team members. Have a bulletin board set aside for staff to post "atta boys" or "atta girls" when they see their fellow staff members go above and beyond. Kudos from customers can be posted, too. We've seen these recognition bulletin boards in hallways, staff lounges, and work areas—spaces that even small facilities can find for this important function.

Celebrate awards, engagements, births, landmarks, and anniversaries; let the staff know you share their happiness. People are people. Although, theoretically, work life and personal life should be separate, realistically, that just isn't the case. Be sensitive to the fact that many people spend as much (or more) time with their coworkers as they do with their families.

Everyone has a birthday. Some libraries have a monthly birthday party to celebrate everyone who has a birthday that month. This avoids constant interruptions to the workflow, particularly in a larger library, where celebrating each birthday would be a bit too much. Some libraries with lots of birthdays choose a time near the end of a month or the beginning of another to celebrate all the birthdays in both months at once. In some libraries, the guest of honor gets the "privilege" of bringing a treat for the entire staff on his or her actual birthday. We like to send an e-card to each staff member. Web sites that offer e-cards make it easy because you can do a bunch of cards at once and program them to be delivered on a specific date. Sometimes we use paper cards and write a special limerick for each celebrant. It doesn't matter how you celebrate the birthdays; it only matters that you do. Most employees really appreciate that the director has remembered their special day. (This works for library board members too!) Again, how you celebrate doesn't really matter; the important thing is that each staff member is afforded some special recognition.

Another occasion that can be celebrated is the person's work anniversary; for example, "On June 4, Mary Fulano will have been working in the library for five years." Likewise, a pizza party to show appreciation for a project well done (such as shifting the nonfiction books) is always appreciated by your team. Keep your eyes open for occasions that may be celebrated, but don't overdo it or they will lose their special meaning.

If you have someone artistic on your staff, you might ask that person to create a poster or bulletin board each month showing all the birthdays and anniversaries that month. The celebrant will appreciate the recognition, and other staff members will appreciate the "heads-up" reminding them to congratulate their colleagues.

Celebrate holidays. Wearing Halloween costumes can be fun. Library patrons, especially the kids, enjoy them. Some librarians even pick a Halloween theme—such as *Pirates of the Caribbean, Lord of the Rings,* or favorite literary characters—and the staff members who choose to participate dress accordingly. Of course, always be sensitive to the staff member who may have ethical or religious reasons for *not* celebrating a particular holiday.

If you have athletes on your staff, they may already be participating in a team sport, such as a city bowling league or town softball team. When they do, thank them for representing the library. Recognize their wins, and commiserate when they lose.

Participating in community events builds teamwork. For example, the library staff might challenge other departments in a firefighter muster (barrel squirt, make and break [laying a hose line, connecting hose sections, and flowing water accurately on target], bucket brigade, hose cart races, waterball, etc.) during your fire department's National Fire Prevention Week celebration. Or if your town has an annual festival, your library might consider having a booth. Many libraries have achieved much goodwill (and national fame within the profession) with a book-cart drill team in the town parade.

Charitable work can also build teamwork. Collecting food for the needy, adopting a family at Christmas, helping with a school clothing/supply drive, or even working together on a house for Habitat for Humanity, creates a sense of working toward something worthwhile as a team. Your group might work the phones at the annual telethon for your local PBS station, perhaps during some of the programming that is sponsored by the American Library Association or your state library association, such as *Reading between the Lions.* We know of at least one library that has established a library charity fund, and every year, they provide Thanksgiving baskets and Christmas toys for families who can't afford such things. Obviously, charitable work can't be mandatory, but you'll likely find that almost everyone will be eager to participate.

Don't be afraid to have fun at the library. Put a puzzle in the employee lounge for staff to work on as they pass through. An ongoing staff-written story on a large piece of paper in the lounge can also provide goofy fun, and you might find out you have some good writers on staff!

PERFORMANCE ACCOUNTABILITY

You have a job to do—providing the best library service possible for your public—and it needs to get done. You need to develop a good working environment for your employees, but you also need to make clear that they are accountable for their actions. A good working environment includes being specific in your expectations and setting goals and objectives for the work team as well as for each staff member.

Don't be afraid to set the bar high. Just because your work environment is friendly and welcoming doesn't mean that you have to accept work that's not up to par. Don't accept "finished" projects until they meet the standards you've established.

Peer pressure can sometimes help people do their best. It's a safe bet that if the standard for shelving books at your library is two carts a shift, and you have someone on your staff who never completes even one cart, other employees will notice. Some will even take it upon themselves to mention it to this person. Of course, you can't (and shouldn't!) rely on peer pressure to fix the problem. Sometimes feedback from peers is a little too enthusiastic and might even be done in an angry manner. Know how you are going to deal with such situations when they reach your ears, and especially how you are going to defuse the anger or jealousy of the other staff members. Learn how to use peer pressure in productive, rather than destructive, ways.

It's possible the person not meeting the quota has been ill, isn't well trained, or has too many other projects. These are things you can address with the employee, but let that person know you need to be informed if there are circumstances preventing him or her from doing a good job. Stress the employee's responsibility to communicate well with you. However, the person who doesn't meet your standards because of poor work habits needs to be told in no uncertain terms that this is not acceptable, as well as what the consequences will be if this substandard performance continues.

Make the staff accountable for the condition of the building. Even if you're in an older building, don't settle for a physical environment that isn't in the best shape possible. Employee committees can nourish accountability, particularly where your library facility is concerned. For example, you might use a committee to attack an ongoing (and possibly universal) problem such as the employee lounge being left in a mess. An unattended lounge area can quickly become the grossest part of the library, and everyone needs to be accountable for its condition. Having staff members take turns serving as hosts will help them develop a feeling of responsibility. One approach is to assign a pair of employees to be hosts of the month. Rotate this assignment so everyone, including yourself, has a turn at the duty. The hosts of the month can keep the lounge area clean and picked up, throw out unrecognizable items from the refrigerator at the end of each month, and get the birthday cards for that month's birthday celebrants. (We've also found it very helpful to post a good-natured sign such as "Your mother doesn't work here; clean up your own mess.")

Another employee committee that can monitor the condition of the library in general is a "Clean Team." Even if you have a custodian, graffiti, torn upholstery, rips in the carpet, and similar signs of wear and tear and vandalism may be ignored, overlooked, or forgotten. The Clean Team inspects the library at regular intervals and lets you know what needs to be done. For example, the best way to prevent a barrage of graffiti is to paint over it or clean it off as soon as it appears. Having people report it immediately so that someone can remove it immediately will go a long way toward alleviating the problem.

Accountability is directly related to the trust factor in your library. It's difficult to work with someone you can't trust. Just as your staff should be able to trust you, you need to be able to trust them. It's hard to have someone on staff you have to constantly remind to finish tasks in a timely fashion, knowing that if you don't, the project won't be done right or at all. It's hard for the rest of the staff, because someone has to pick up the work the other person didn't feel compelled to do, and that's just not fair! If you want to create discord among staff (we hope you don't!), all you have to do is permit an atmosphere of real or perceived unfairness.

EVALUATING STAFF

Feedback from supervisors is essential for employees, especially positive feedback. Feedback should be an ongoing process. An employee should *never* be taken by surprise by his or her annual evaluation.

No one has a perfect memory. Keep notes for that time of year when you fill out evaluation forms. For example: "On March 9, you received a written thank-you from Ms. Cassell for going above and beyond in helping her find materials and resources for her unit on citizenship."

Use corrective feedback, not soul-crushing criticism. Tone and choice of words can set an employee into a self-defeating spiral. You want to correct the employee's behavior or performance, not damage that person's self-esteem so badly that he or she will worry about ever living up to any standard, let alone yours.

Employee recognition is important. Studies have shown that feeling appreciated is more important to employees than monetary compensation. Praise a job well done. Use sincere praise, and lots of it. Be as specific as possible. An example of this might be, "You did a great job organizing that program on diabetes. You followed up with the speakers, and your press release was picked up by the media. Good work!" Be sure to acknowledge this success at your next staff meeting and mention it to your supervisor as well as in your employee's review.

EVALUATING YOURSELF

How are *you* doing? Encourage honest feedback from staff. "Yes men" (and women) can only mean you've multiplied your own deficiencies, sometimes exponentially.

Try a 360-degree evaluation. In a 360-degree evaluation, you get feedback from your supervisor, your peers, people you supervise, and customers. Some people are threatened by this kind of evaluation, but there's really nothing to fear. You will get positive comments, but be prepared for some constructive criticism; there are apt to be suggestions you can put to use. You may even receive some criticism that is not so constructive. Part of being a supervisor is being able to deal with that type of thing and learn from it. Remedy the negative and stay focused on the positive. Your goal is to improve yourself, not sink in discouragement.

THE GOLDEN RULE

Treat people like you want to be treated. Following this one tenet will make you a better supervisor than many people who have much more experience than you. Think about some bad supervisors you have had and make a concerted effort *not* to be like that.

- You don't like to be yelled at? Don't yell at your staff.
- You don't like people to ignore what you have to say? Listen to your staff.
- You don't like to be around people who are so capricious that you never know where you stand with them? Be consistent with your staff.
- You don't like to be kept in the dark? Keep communications open.

Some extraordinary people are able to follow the Platinum Rule: "Do unto others as they would have you do unto them." If you are fortunate enough to have these empathetic people on staff, count your lucky stars. If you're one of these people, your staff is fortunate indeed! To become such a person, you must be perceptive. Be sensitive to your staff and try to learn how they would like to be treated. Be observant. Then, put into practice what you have learned.

SMILING: A PRICELESS TOOL

Smile!

A cheerful supervisor sets the tone for the workplace. People should love to come to work. They should enjoy their jobs. Have you ever been in a position where the supervisor was so cranky and negative that you had to force yourself to go to work? Lead by example.

Your staff and volunteers need to understand that they will, at one time or another, be the very first point of contact for the public, and a smiling, friendly attitude is imperative. One library supervisor tells her staff, "Check your frowns at the door and pick up your smile." (Of course, they won't be able to do this if you haven't created a positive work environment.)

The private (for-profit) sector recognizes the value of smiling. One large business gave its employees mirrored pencil holders for their desks so they could check their smiles, instructing them to smile when they answered the phone...because it showed in their voices.

Remember that song from *Annie,* "You're Never Fully Dressed without a Smile"? The title alone would make a great motto for library managers and directors and their staffs.

THE IMPORTANCE OF FAIRNESS AND CONSISTENCY

Your staff needs to know, or at least guess fairly accurately, how you're going to react in any given situation. If someone makes a mistake and you tell that person, "It's okay, just fix it," and then you literally scream at the next person who does the same thing, you'll drive your staff crazy.

Yes, you're human. Yes, your mood will change. But be consistent in dealing with your staff. Do your best to leave your outside problems outside the workplace.

Follow through; don't make empty promises. If you've told your staff that you're going to do something, do it. If you can't do it, or if you change your mind, explain that to your staff.

Do you expect loyalty from your staff? That's a two-way street. Being fair and consistent will help pave it.

ETHICAL LEADERSHIP

Are you an ethical person?

A good rule of thumb is to ask yourself, "If what I'm about to do were to appear in tomorrow's newspaper, what would people think?" A more personal test for those with a functional conscience is, "Will I be able to look myself in the mirror if I do this?"

As a manager, it's your responsibility to make sure that the directives you receive from above are carried through. As an ethical person, you'll want to be certain these orders are ethical, moral, and legal. If you're not comfortable with something that you or your staff have been told to do, question it. If this begins to happen on a regular basis, you need to ask yourself if you're a good fit with the organization. Sometimes you may need to become a whistleblower.

AVOID OSTRICH MANAGEMENT

If there's a problem and you ignore it, it won't go away. It will only get bigger. Deal with problems head-on. Someone once said that an ostrich makes a better target when it has its head in the sand.

MAINTAIN A ZERO TOLERANCE POLICY FOR RACISM AND SEXUAL HARASSMENT

Besides being illegal and just plain wrong, racism, sexism, and so forth have no place in your library. Neither does sexual harassment. Intolerance and discrimination of any kind should be dealt with immediately. Make sure your staff receives diversity training as well as training on how to avoid committing sexual harassment and on what to do should they become a victim. Not dealing with such a situation appropriately and immediately could cost you your job and potentially have additional legal repercussions.

SHARE THE CREDIT

Have you ever worked hard on a project and produced an excellent result, only to have someone else take credit for it? We have. Supervisors who take the credit for what members of their staff have done will find themselves on a steep, slippery slope. And the loyalty factor from the people they supervise will be a big, fat zero. Always share credit. It's the right thing to do.

ADMIT WHEN YOU'RE WRONG

You're only human, and we can guarantee you'll make a mistake. It might be a little one, or it could even be career threatening. No matter what, you need to admit when you're wrong. If you pretend you're not at fault when you are, or worse yet, if you try to shift the blame to some innocent staff member, you will lose the respect of your staff, not to mention your self-respect. It's important to remember that if there are problems at the library, the buck stops with you. You definitely don't want to get the reputation of being a Teflon supervisor!

THE MYTH OF CONTROL

Many new supervisors have the mistaken idea that they can control their staff at all times. Control, like Jason and the Argonauts, is a myth. Anyone who's ever been married, had children, or owned a cat already knows this. Trying to stay in control 100 percent of the time is an impossible task and can only add incredible stress to your life, not to mention your staff's. You become a micromanager, and your staff will dread every minute you're hovering over them.

IN SUMMARY

A good manager or director should have excellent communication skills, including the ability to listen to others. The manager should be aware of personnel rules and follow them at all times. Good administrators have superior leadership abilities and strong ethics. They have high expectations and lead by example. They build teams, set the bar high, hold their staff accountable, share credit, and do their best to be fair and consistent. But no one's perfect, and the ability to admit error and apologize when wrong sets the truly great administrators apart from the rest of their peers.

NOTE

1. Patrick Lencioni, *The Five Dysfunctions of a Team: A Leadership Fable* (San Francisco: Jossey-Bass, 2000).

CHAPTER 4

Personnel Laws: You Can't Become Familiar with These Too Quickly or Too Soon!

It may be true that the law cannot make a man love me, but it can stop him from lynching me, and I think that's pretty important.
—Dr. Martin Luther King Jr. (1929–1968)

Okay. You've gotten to know the human resources (personnel) director. You've almost memorized the employee handbook. You have your very own copy of your organization's human resources/personnel rules—and you're following them.

You're all set. Right? Wrong. You need to know about all sorts of state and federal labor laws. Some of them even need to be on permanent display in your facility. Check with your organization's human resources department to see which of these laws need to be posted in your library. That department should have the necessary flyers and posters.

The U.S. Department of Labor is the agency that oversees the compliance of more than 180 labor laws. Their Web site at www.dol.

31

gov/elaws explains many of the laws mentioned in this chapter. This Web site's virtual counseling and plethora of information will help you understand your rights and responsibilities under the regulations and laws that are administered by the Department of Labor.

This chapter, like chapter 5, is meant strictly as a guideline and is based on our experience. It is not intended to be used for legal advice. Directors may not be lawyers, but it is extremely important that they be aware of the legal framework within which they operate.

AFFIRMATIVE ACTION

Affirmative Action is a program designed to combat discrimination against women and minorities. Developed to rectify hundreds of years of racial and gender discrimination, Affirmative Action includes the recruitment and advancement of qualified minorities, women, disabled people, and certain veterans. Based on the concept that people with equal abilities should have equal opportunities, Affirmative Action includes training and outreach efforts. Organizations set goals and timetables for increased diversity using such strategies as targeted recruitment (e.g., in minority newspapers) to meet them. An employer faced with two equally qualified applicants might select a minority candidate over a Caucasian, or a woman instead of a man. Opponents of Affirmative Action have called it "reverse discrimination," but without it, who knows where women and minorities would be in today's workforce?

AGE DISCRIMINATION IN EMPLOYMENT ACT (ADEA)

The Age Discrimination in Employment Act (ADEA) prohibits employers from discriminating against employees because of their age. This protected age group starts at age 40. The ADEA is enforced by the Equal Employment Opportunity Commission (EEOC).

In our experience, we have found that older workers are often outstanding employees. They tend to have an excellent work ethic and take pride in their work. We have had reference librarians in their late 70s and pages in their 60s on our staffs, and they were model employees.

AMERICANS WITH DISABILITIES ACT (ADA)

The Americans with Disabilities Act (ADA) is legislation that prohibits discrimination against a person on the basis of a disability. It requires that employers make their facilities accessible as well as provide reasonable accommodation for employees with disabilities. The ADA is enforced by the EEOC.

CIVIL RIGHTS LAWS

Civil rights legislation prohibits employers from discriminating against their employees on the basis of race, color, religion, sex, or national origin. Enforcement is overseen by the Civil Rights Division of the U.S. Department of Justice.

DRUG-FREE WORKPLACE

In 1988, the Drug-Free Workplace Act was passed, requiring employers to provide a drug-free, alcohol-free workplace if they were contractors or received federal grants. The requirements soon became part of state, county, and municipal workplace standards. In order to prevent substance abuse in the workplace, a drug-screening policy was also put into place.

If you supervise for any amount of time at all, you are very likely to run across an employee who has a substance-abuse problem. However, you'll find that the drug-free workplace requirements aren't as black and white as they seem. For example, alcoholism is sometimes considered a disease, and some human resources departments treat an employee abusing alcohol as someone who has a disability.

EMPLOYEE POLYGRAPH PROTECTION ACT (EPPA)

Administered by the Wage and Hour Division of the Department of Labor, the Employee Polygraph Protection Act of 1988 bars most employers from using lie detector tests on employees, whether it's part of their preemployment screening or during employment. However, there are some exemptions, and certain polygraph, or lie detector, tests may be administered in limited circumstances. For the most part, employees may not be disciplined, terminated, or discriminated against if they refuse to submit to a polygraph. The EPPA poster is one of those that employers are required to post in the workplace for their employees' information.

You might be thinking to yourself that the EPPA is something that would never affect you as a director. So did we, until we had some money stolen from the library safe. All employees (most of whom had worked there for years) at that facility were subjected to lie detector tests, which included some extremely humiliating and personal questions. One person was even put on administrative leave with pay. Morale took a nosedive, and staff wondered why the trust factor was suddenly gone. In the end, it turned out that a cleaning contractor had figured out how to get into the safe. It was a long time before the hard feelings that resulted from this episode were smoothed over.

EMPLOYMENT AND TRAINING ADMINISTRATION (ETA)

The Employment and Training Administration (ETA) directs federal-government job training, oversees worker dislocation programs, provides federal grants to the individual states for public-employment service programs, and administers unemployment insurance benefits. Although a federal agency, the ETA provides its services through state and local workforce development systems.

EMPLOYMENT STANDARDS ADMINISTRATION (ESA)

Part of the Department of Labor, the Employment Standards Administration (ESA) has the mission to "enhance the welfare and protect the rights of American workers." The ESA has four major programs: the Office of Federal Contract Compliance Programs, the Office of Labor-Management Standards, the Office of Workers' Compensation Programs, and the Wage and Hour Division.

EQUAL EMPLOYMENT OPPORTUNITY COMMISSION (EEOC)

The EEOC consists of five commissioners and a general counsel appointed by the president of the United States and confirmed by the U.S. Senate. The members of the commission make policy regarding equal employment opportunity and approve most litigation. The EEOC enforces antidiscrimination laws: Title VII of the Civil Rights Act of 1964 (Title VII), the Equal Pay Act (EPA), the Age Discrimination in Employment Act (ADEA), and the Americans with Disabilities Act (ADA).

EQUAL PAY ACT (EPA)

The Equal Pay Act of 1963 (EPA), mandates equal pay for equal work. In other words, an employer cannot pay a male worker more than a female worker doing the same job. Likewise, if two workers are employed in jobs requiring the same level of skill, effort, responsibility, and working conditions, an employer cannot pay a male employee more than a female employee just because of the difference in gender. The EPA is enforced by the EEOC.

FAIR LABOR STANDARDS ACT (FLSA)

The Fair Labor Standards Act of 1938 (FLSA) sets standards for wages and overtime pay. It requires employers to pay nonexempt employees at least the federal minimum wage and overtime pay of 1.5 times their regular rate of pay for all time worked over 40 hours in a work week. It also deals with child labor, restricting the hours that children under age 16 can work and forbidding the employment of children under the age of 18 in jobs that are dangerous.

Hourly employees are nonexempt (that is, not exempt from the FLSA), but some of your salaried staff might be nonexempt, too. That means when they work overtime, they get compensated for it. Using exemption tests (salary level, salary basis, standard duties) your organization's human resources department will determine who's exempt and who's not exempt from the FLSA's minimum wage and overtime pay requirements. Your job is to know who on your staff is and isn't exempt. You need to know which work-related activities coming before or after the workday are considered "hours worked," hours for which these employees must be paid additional compensation.

FAMILY AND MEDICAL LEAVE ACT (FMLA)

The Wage and Hour Division also administers and enforces the Family and Medical Leave Act (FMLA), which provides up to 12 weeks of unpaid, job-protected leave per year to eligible employees for specified family and medical reasons and requires that group health benefits be maintained during the leave. Reasons for this leave include the birth or adoption of a child or the serious illness of the employee, spouse, child, or parent.

As director, you should be familiar with eligibility and valid reasons for taking leave, how to designate and schedule the leave, notification and record-keeping responsibilities on your part and that of the employee, and employee rights and benefits under the FMLA. For follow-up, you need to know the requirements for benefit continuation as well as job restoration. Record keeping is a major component of complying with the FMLA. Work closely with your organization's human resources department when an employee requests leave under the FMLA.

GARNISHMENT OF WAGES

An employee's check can be garnished for various reasons. The Consumer Credit Protection Act (also administered by the Department of Labor's Wage and Hour Division) regulates the garnishment of an employee's wages by employers. Reasons for garnishment may include money owed for debts or back payments of child or spousal support.

HEALTH INSURANCE PORTABILITY AND ACCOUNTABILITY ACT (HIPAA)

If you've been to see your doctor since April 14, 2003, you're probably familiar with HIPAA and the mountains of paperwork it entails. HIPAA is more than protected health information (PHI). It's also federal legislation that provides rights for participants and their beneficiaries in group plans. Under this act, exclusion based on pre-existing conditions is limited. Employees and their dependents can't be discriminated against because of the status of their health. With HIPAA, employees and their families can make informed decisions about employer-based health benefits, particularly when they face life-changing events such as marriage, divorce, childbirth, adoption, divorce, or death. This is also true when an employee faces job loss or retirement or moves to a new job. Under certain circumstances, HIPAA allows employees to enroll in other plans, purchase individual insurance, or obtain insurance when their COBRA (bridge insurance) benefits run out.

HOSTILE WORK ENVIRONMENT

In a hostile work environment, an employee dreads going to work because a harasser (or harassers) has created an intimidating, unpleasant, threatening, odious, and/or oppressive atmosphere in the workplace. Just about anyone can create a hostile work environment: directors, managers, supervisors, coworkers, or even customers and outside vendors. The harassment constitutes a violation of a person's civil rights and can be based on that person's race, color, ancestry, ethnicity, nationality, citizenship status, political affiliation, gender, sexual orientation, religion or creed, physical handicap/disability, medical condition, personal appearance, marital status, veteran status, or education. In a hostile work environment, an employee is unable to function well and can't do the job. The harassment can be done through speech and/or conduct. It can involve vandalism or discriminatory job assignments. Much harassment that takes place in a hostile work environment is sexual in nature and can consist of the use of sexual language, innuendo, or lewd or vulgar jokes or comments; sexual materials, including posters and cartoons; or unwelcome, unwanted physical contact, such as touching or fondling.

As director, it's your job to prevent a hostile work environment. It's not bad just for the person who's being harassed; it's bad for the whole library.

OCCUPATIONAL SAFETY AND HEALTH ACT (OSHA)

The Occupational Safety and Health Act of 1970 (OSHA) establishes safety and health standards for the workplace. Under OSHA, employers have to provide their employees with a safe workplace, free from hazards. Your library may be inspected by the Occupational Safety and Health Administration (also OSHA), but if they find violations, they will also offer compliance advice or assistance.

Your janitor's or custodian's closet is an example of something that has been affected by workplace safety regulations. Material Safety Data Sheets (MSDSs) need to be posted for each chemical solution used in your library for such purposes as cleaning. Never underestimate the damage a chemical can do to a facility and the people in it. At one of our libraries, a building maintenance worker on a mission to eradicate some new graffiti sprayed the exterior with a strong chemical solution. Unfortunately, he sprayed right by the air intake vents. Fumes filled the library, and both patrons and staff, most coughing and a few gagging, had to be evacuated from the building. The MSDS information showed that the cleaner had a benzene base, so we were able to tell the people affected what the fumes were.

SEXUAL HARASSMENT

Sexual harassment is unwanted, unwelcome sexual advances, innuendos, touching, inappropriate jokes, and so forth in the workplace, especially by someone in a position of authority. Sexual harassment is a serious offense and must be treated with a zero tolerance policy. As director, you need to make sure your staff is trained to avoid and prevent sexual harassment as well as communicate to you immediately should it happen. It doesn't always have to be explicit in nature. Some not-so-obvious behaviors may be considered sexual harassment in a court of law. If a person's behavior makes another person feel uncomfortable, even if the person doesn't say anything at the time, it can still be grounds for harassment. For example, if you're the only woman in a group of men telling off-color jokes, you may not feel comfortable telling them to stop, or fear you may be harassed further if you do. But later you might file a complaint. In some cases, such complaints have been upheld by the courts as sexual harassment.

TITLE VII

Title VII, also known as Title VII of the Civil Rights Act of 1964, is one of the major civil rights bills. It is enforced by the EEOC.

TITLE 29

If you want to find what the labor laws are and what agencies are responsible for them, Title 29 of the U.S. Code is a one-stop place for information. For an indexed copy of Title 29, see the web site of the Cornell Law School: www.law.cornell.edu/uscode/html/uscode29/usc_sup_01_29.html.

UNIFORMED SERVICES EMPLOYMENT AND REEMPLOYMENT RIGHTS ACT (USERRA)

Certain persons who serve in the armed forces have a right to reemployment with their previous employer when they return from service, including those in the Reserves or National Guard. As director, you need to understand their rights and responsibilities under USERRA.

UNIONS AND THEIR MEMBERS

The Landrum-Griffin Act (Labor-Management Reporting and Disclosure Act of 1959) deals with unions and their members. It mandates that labor organizations file annual financial reports; requires union officials, employers, and labor consultants to file reports regarding certain labor relations practices; and establishes standards for the election of union officers.

One librarian left an Arizona library to become a director in California. The Arizona library wasn't unionized, but the California library was. She had to learn a whole set of rules and regulations to enable her to be a manager in a union shop. This is only one of many possible differences you can encounter when you accept a position as a director in another state or even another area. If you're new to this area, make sure you're aware of local laws and regulations.

VETERANS' EMPLOYMENT AND TRAINING SERVICE (VETS)

Part of the Department of Labor, the Veterans' Employment and Training Service (VETS), provides veterans, Reservists, National Guard, and transitioning service members with the resources and services necessary to succeed in the workforce and protects their employment rights. This includes preference in hiring and protection during layoffs or reductions in force (RIFs).

WHISTLEBLOWER PROTECTION

OSHA enforces whistleblower protection in most labor and public safety laws and many environmental laws. These protections are in place for employees who complain or turn in their employers for violating the law. A wrongfully terminated whistleblower can have his or her job reinstated and receive back wages.

WOMEN'S BUREAU (WB)

The Women's Bureau (WB) sets standards and policies to "promote the welfare of wage-earning women, improve their working conditions, increase their efficiency, and advance their opportunities for profitable employment." The WB performs investigations as to the welfare of women in industry, the results of which may be published.

WORKPLACE VIOLENCE

Terminated employees returning to their former workplace with assault weapons, rejected suitors killing everyone in their would-be lover's office disgruntled employees sending letter bombs: The daily newspapers are filled with examples of workplace violence. Violence in the workplace is a serious issue for employers and employees alike. In the United States, the most extreme form of workplace violence, homicide, is the third-leading cause of fatal occupational injury. Environmental conditions associated with workplace assaults have been identified, and control strategies implemented, in a number of work settings.

Volunteers and patrons can also display violent behavior in he workplace. When a certain volunteer was placed at our library for training, his caseworker never indicated that when not medicated, the volunteer was prone to violent behavior. One day, we found that out the hard way. The volunteer had neglected to take his medicine for several days, and once in the library workroom, he "snapped," grabbing scissors from the book mending station and brandishing them at everyone in sight. He knocked over book carts and furniture and began throwing things. Fortunately, no one was hurt. Incredible as it might seem, his caseworker wanted us to reinstate him.

As director, you need to have a zero tolerance policy toward workplace violence. Your employees need to be trained to recognize behaviors and situations that could end in workplace violence. Their training should also include ways to prevent violence and the confrontations that can lead to violence. Don't ever delude yourself into thinking that because it's a library, it's a safe haven.

IN SUMMARY

You don't have to be a lawyer to be a library director, though it could help. But you must understand that libraries operate within a given legal framework. It is the director's responsibility to know pertinent laws and how to function within them. Make sure you are well acquainted with your organization's legal counsel, and don't hesitate to call on that person when doubts arise. If possible, keep a copy of the necessary laws close at hand or, at least, know where to get them quickly.

CHAPTER 5

Hiring, Firing, and Other Good Stuff: It Happens Even if You're New!

> The seven deadly sins...Food, clothing, firing, rent, taxes, respectability and children. Nothing can lift those seven millstones from man's neck but money; and the spirit cannot soar until the millstones are lifted.
>
> —George Bernard Shaw (1856–1950)

Library operations don't slow down as soon as you begin your job as director to give you a chance to learn the ropes. Life keeps going on, sometimes at what appears to be breakneck speed. Personnel actions and disciplinary measures can take place early in your tenure, and it's vital that you perform these in a fair and legal manner.

This chapter, like chapter 4, is meant strictly as a guideline, and is based on our experience. It is not intended to be used for legal advice. Directors may not be lawyers, but it is extremely important that they be aware of the legal framework within which they operate.

RECRUITING STAFF

Staff openings occur for many reasons: resignations, terminations, retirements, transfers, medical problems, and unfortunately, even death. The first thing you need to do with an open position is to analyze the job. Ideally, some type of job description will already exist, but if not, work with your staff to make a list of duties the person in that position performed. Sometimes, the job title and description don't match the list of actual duties. What needs changing: the duties or the title? You might even find that you need to shift that position to another area of the library. You need to work with your organization's human resources department to create the criteria for that position: education, experience, and KSAs (knowledge, skills, and abilities).

Once you decide what attributes a person in that position requires, you need to decide how long you can function with that position vacant. This and the amount of time human resources takes to process your position will determine your recruitment deadline.

You might have good in-house candidates, and they should always be considered, but maybe you want to open up the pool of applicants. You want a good pool of candidates to choose from, diverse and qualified. You want to target and find the ideal candidate. Post this position in as many places as you can afford:

- Your library's Web site
- Your organization's (town, city, etc.) Web site
- Bulletin boards throughout the organization
- Local newspapers
- Local cable television
- Minority newspapers
- State library hotline
- State library association hotline
- Professional journals and their Web sites, such as jobs.libraryjournal.com
- Library schools
- Web sites for online job seekers, such as www.monster.com and hotjobs.yahoo.com
- The American Library Association Web site, joblist.ala.org (for a fee)
- Library-focused job-seeker Web sites such as www.libjobs.com and www.lisjobs.com
- Web sites from local library networks such as www.baynetlibs.org/jobs/jobs_index.html

Other information channels exist for advertising your position. These include word of mouth from happy employees and sharing information about the position with your colleagues, who may know of interested job seekers.

THE SELECTION PROCESS

Hopefully, once you've advertised your position, you'll have a good pool of applicants. As a courtesy to the applicants, acknowledge the receipt of their applications. Even a postcard is okay. Some libraries use a preprinted card or one-page form with checkboxes showing which items have been received and which are still missing. E-mail notification is becoming increasingly common, particularly for applications that have been submitted electronically.

Before you and/or human resources screen the applications, prepare a matrix based on the research you did about the position. This should include the minimum qualifications (MQs) needed to perform the work the job requires. The matrix should include such criteria as a minimum educational requirement, a minimum number of years of library experience, and whether or not experience in supervision is needed.

Once the applications are screened, it's time to make preparations for the selection interviews. You need to put together a team to interview and screen the candidates. Choose your interview team wisely. Obviously, interview-team members need to know something about the position and they need to understand the screening process; if not, you will have to train them. Your organization's human resources department might have specific guidelines on the composition of a team, but if they don't, try to include someone from your staff, a person or two from an outside library, and a representative from human resources. If this position is in a specific department or work area of the library, include someone from that area. The supervisor of this position should definitely be on the team. As director, you might choose to either sit on the team or wait and interview the team's top two or three candidates.

Questions for the interviewees should be prepared before the interviews. In fairness and to make sure you are on solid legal footing for hiring, be sure to ask all the candidates the same questions. During the process, the team members may ask follow-up questions to clarify a candidate's answers; these are situational and do not need to be the same for all candidates. Don't prompt candidates on their answers. Team members need to be aware of the legalities of the hiring process and that they may not ask questions regarding topics such as religion, political viewpoints, or marital status. For example, asking an out-of-town candidate, "How do you think your family would like living here?" may seem like an innocent question, but it is strictly a "no-no."

Questions for the candidates sometimes need to be preapproved by the human resources department to make sure what you're asking is legal. For example, asking candidates if they have any problems working on Saturdays might give the impression that you are discriminating against such religious groups as Jews or Seventh Day Adventists. Asking candidates when they graduated from high school is tantamount to asking how old they are, something else it's not legal to do. You also can't ask a candidate about, for example, his or her health, ethnicity, or marital status.

Questions for candidates might include the following:

- "Why do you want to work at this particular library?" The answer to this question will show you who cared enough to do their homework and learn about your library ahead of time.
- "Do you like working with the public? Please give us some examples of situations when your customer service skills were outstanding."
- "Where do you see yourself in five years?" A technical services manager actually had a candidate answer, "Doing your job." It's amazing what people say during their interviews!
- "What computer hardware and software are you comfortable using?" In this day and age, you don't want to hire someone who's technologically illiterate.
- "What did you do in your last position to improve service to the public?" This is a good way to gauge creativity as well as commitment to customer service. Maybe the candidate started a storytime for seniors in nursing homes or an adult summer reading program or a "teen corner."
- "What would you do if a patron started yelling at you in the public area of the library?" The response to this gives you a glimpse of what this person would do under pressure.
- "How do you most like to be supervised?" "How do you like to supervise?" "How would you describe your style of management?" The responses to this set of questions can sometimes prevent you from hiring a micromanager or someone who resents being supervised.
- "Do you prefer to work as part of a team or by yourself? Why?" Sometimes, the response is "I like to work both

ways," which shouldn't raise any red flags. However, if teams are the modus operandi in your library, watch out for the person who replies that he or she can't stand working in a team because of some bad previous experience and only wants to fly solo.

- "Describe a time when you worked on a successful team." "What role did you play?" "What made the team successful?" This works well as a follow-up to the previous question.
- "Have you ever worked with a difficult person? Describe that person and what you did to facilitate working relations."
- "Tell us about a time you worked under a lot of pressure because of a strict deadline or a sudden increase in your workload." You can follow this up with "How did you react to that situation?" or "Have you ever missed a deadline? Why?" "How did you deal with it?"
- "Did you ever work on a project that had lots of roadblocks and obstacles? How did you deal with these?" Anyone can finish a slam-dunk project. You want someone who's had to have the persistence, resourcefulness, and determination to see a project to completion when the odds were against him or her.
- "Have you ever multitasked?" "How do you handle multiple projects?" Since working in a library is one big multiple project, the response to this is very important.
- "How do you ensure that your work is accurate?" Accuracy is vital in a library. Errors can unintentionally send people to collection agencies, lose books forever, and destroy public confidence. Some interview teams follow up with the question, "How many errors are acceptable while you're working the circulation/reference/youth/technical services desks?"
- "How would you describe yourself?"
- "What three words would your previous supervisors use to describe you?"
- "What three words would your coworkers use to describe you?"

A few more tips for a successful interview process:

- Also use the interview time to ask candidates to clarify any questions you have about their application and résumé.
- Give yourself at least 45 minutes for each interview, with at least 15 minutes between each candidate.

- Out of courtesy to the candidates, keep them separate; if necessary, bring them in one door and out another.
- Make sure the break between them is sufficient that they won't encounter each other, even if an interview runs long or the next candidate arrives early. You might have two candidates from the same library and neither one knows that the other is job hunting!
- Don't rush the process. Remember that you are not only determining the future of the library, but what you do may have lifelong implications for the candidate. Some decisions require more than an hour or two, so take all the time you need. For a higher-level position, it may be a two-day process.
- Be sure the interview-team members have breaks, and provide snacks, drinks, and lunch for them if the interviewing lasts all day.

In addition to the formal interview with the selection team, some libraries add other steps to the process, such as an open forum, particularly for higher-level positions such as managers or department heads. During an open forum, all available staff members are encouraged to come meet the candidate. Sometimes the candidate will be asked to make a formal presentation during this time. The presentation might be on a specific topic, such as the candidate's views on exceptional public service, or just a brief introduction of him- or herself to the group. During the forum, staff members are given the opportunity to ask the candidate anything they'd like. Naturally, staff must be given guidelines before the forum as to what types of questions are and are not legal. (Food is always a good incentive to encourage staff to attend the forum.)

FORCED RANKING FOR APPLICANTS DURING THE JOB INTERVIEW PROCESS

You've narrowed the applicants down to five people to be interviewed, prepared the questions to ask them, and (for purposes of our example) have decided to interview them in alphabetical order: Larry Anderson, Ana Garcia, Mark Jones, Tamara Lee, and Lydia Patel. But how will you pick your top candidate? There are many ways to rank candidates, but this forced ranking system is our favorite.

On the day of the interviews, in addition to a set of questions, give each interview-team member a form in the following format:

1.	1.	1.	1.	1.
	2.	2.	2.	2.
		3.	3.	3.
			4.	4.
				5.

Your first interview is with Larry Anderson. Larry Anderson is an average sort of candidate. He has the credentials but gives unimpressive answers to the questions. However, no matter how well or poorly Larry Anderson does, he's the number one candidate until the next person is interviewed.

1. Anderson	1.	1.	1.	1.
	2.	2.	2.	2.
		3.	3.	3.
			4.	4.
				5.

Your second interview is with Ana Garcia. Ana Garcia answers the questions better than Larry Anderson did, and she has quite a bit more experience. She goes into the number one spot, and Larry Anderson moves to number two.

1. Anderson	1. Garcia	1.	1.	1.
	2. Anderson	2.	2.	2.
		3.	3.	3.
			4.	4.
				5.

Your third interview is with Mark Jones. Mark Jones doesn't impress you as much as either Ana Garcia or Larry Anderson, so he goes into third place.

1. Anderson	1. Garcia	1. Garcia	1.	1.
	2. Anderson	2. Anderson	2.	2.
		3. Jones	3.	3.
			4.	4.
				5.

Your fourth interview is with Tamara Lee. Tamara Lee is unapologetically late to the interview. She knows nothing about your organization and missed all but one of the technical questions during the interview. You wonder to yourself how she got through the initial screening, let alone library school. She's easily in last place, so you write her name by number four.

1. Anderson	1. Garcia	1. Garcia	1. Garcia	1.
	2. Anderson	2. Anderson	2. Anderson	2.
		3. Jones	3. Jones	3.
			4. Lee	4.
				5.

Your fifth and final interview is with Lydia Patel. She gave the best answers to your questions. She has extensive experience and has shown a lot of enthusiasm as well as a sense of humor during the interview. She's also researched your library and has been very specific in her reasons to want to work with you. Lydia Patel is now your number one choice. The other candidates move down one spot.

1. Anderson	1. Garcia	1. Garcia	1. Garcia	1. Patel
	2. Anderson	2. Anderson	2. Anderson	2. Garcia
		3. Jones	3. Jones	3. Anderson
			4. Lee	4. Jones
				5. Lee

You've finished ranking the candidates, but you withhold discussion with other interview-team members until they've finished their own rankings. As the results are tallied, it's obvious that Lydia Patel and Ana Garcia are everyone's first- and second-place choices. Of course, there is that rare occasion when a given candidate is all over the place on the various team members' rankings. At that point, each team member needs to discuss the reasons for his or her scoring. The candidate's qualifications and responses to the interview question also need to be examined more closely.

There are other ways to rank candidates during an interview, including assigning a point value to each answer, totaling the points, then averaging the interview team members' results. We like the forced ranking system because there's usually no question as to who ranks number one and number two.

To maintain the integrity of the process, the interview team needs to be instructed that they are not to discuss their decisions after leaving the interview room. All discussions among interview-team members remain behind closed doors.

ONCE YOU HAVE AN IDEA WHO YOU WANT TO HIRE...

- *Checking references.* Call the top candidate's previous supervisors as well as the people that person has listed as personal references. Have a list of questions to ask each reference and jot down the responses. Sample questions might include, "If you could hire this person, would you? Why or why not?" "Is there anything I haven't asked about that you think we need to know?" Here's the caveat: In recent years, many organizations have set strict rules as to what a person can or cannot say about a former employee. In fact, don't be surprised if you're redirected to the human resources department, who will tell you only the candidate's dates of employment.

- *Reviewing your decision.* Look at the successful candidate's application and résumé again. Examine the notes of the interview team and others who may have had input into the process, such as those who attended the open forum. Assess the responses from the reference check. When you're sure you have the best person for the job, inform the human resources department and your supervisor of your decision.

- *Notifying the unsuccessful candidates.* Sometimes, human resources does this, but sometimes, you get to be the bearer of bad news. Do it in a timely manner, as soon as the successful candidate has accepted your offer. These applicants don't like waiting for an answer any more than you did when you applied for your job. Be a bit cautious, however. If the hiring isn't final until board approval, wait until after the next board meeting; things do sometimes go awry.

- *Making the offer.* Delivering the good news is the best part of the process. Of course, it's good news for the selected candidate, but it's also good news for the library because you've now filled your position and the labor of the search process is behind you.

Whatever your jurisdiction (county, township, city, state, tribe, etc.) there are bound to be rules about the hiring process. There are also very specific federal laws (details in chapter 4) that *must* be followed. You should be familiar with these. Things to consider:

- The candidate has to meet the minimum requirements of the job in terms of education and experience. In some cases, human resources will determine if there is an "equivalency" (more education than required may offset less experience, or vice versa).
- The candidate may not be discriminated against on the basis of ethnicity, religion, race, sex, age, or disability.
- If the candidate has a disability, take into account that he or she can often do the job with "reasonable accommodation." In other words, if a qualified candidate uses a wheelchair and your worktable isn't high enough to accommodate it, that person still needs to be considered. You can make reasonable accommodation by raising the existing table or adding a higher table to the work area. If a qualified person has lupus and can't tolerate sunshine, but the work area is by a sunny table, you can move the table or put a shade on the window. In both of these cases, accommodating the potential candidate is both easy and doable. The accommodation is reasonable and, by law, the candidate must be considered and the accommodation made.
- Nepotism, or hiring a relative, can lead to problems within the workplace. Rules on nepotism vary from place to place and should be part of your board's policy. Make sure that you and everyone in your library is familiar with these rules.

TRAINING NEW HIRES AND OTHER STAFF

Once a person is hired, training is vital and needs to be ongoing for all staff. Training keeps staff current with policies and technologies. It helps them keep up with trends and developments. It keeps staff apprised of personnel rules. It can help prevent discipline problems.

Sometimes directors complain that they're expected to train staff with little or no professional development budget. They see big conferences and expensive seminars as the only paths to true professional development. (Then sometimes when they do have money for conferences, they use it all on themselves, but that's another story.) Professional development and training can start in-house. Here are some free and low-cost options:

- *Mentoring.* Management guru Tom Peters once said, "Leaders don't create followers, they create more leaders." Mentoring is more than training. It involves developing a long-term relationship with mentees, encouraging their professional growth, and showing them the ropes. Usually, a mentoring relationship is for a predetermined period of time, such as a year or two. It may be a formal or informal process. Some librarians define the tasks a mentor is supposed to accomplish. In other libraries, it's the mentor's simply being available for any issues the new employee would like help with.

- *One-on-one training.* This is short-term and teaches specific skills. For example, someone may train the new employee on the proper procedures for working the circulation desk.

- *Group training.* Some skills, such as the use of new databases or reference works, lend themselves to group training. If there's a lot of information presented, distribute a "cheat sheet" to refresh your staff's memory later. Always allow some time after the training for staff to experiment with their new resources. Remember that training must be timely. If staff can't immediately apply what they have learned, they will forget. If they are trained too early, the training will be theoretical and meaningless and won't be retained. If their training is delayed, they may pick up bad habits that are hard to break.

- *Retreats.* Retreats get you and your staff away from the library so you can look at successes and issues in a neutral area. Many restaurants have meeting rooms you can use at no charge if your staff eats a meal there. Some library directors use the meeting rooms of neighboring libraries for their retreats. Retreats need to be booked and planned in advance. Be sure to include some fun team-building activities!

- *Cross-training.* If you have a small staff, reference staff might have to work at the circulation desk occasionally, for example. Youth services staff may be called on to work reference. People have personal business to attend to. People go on vacation. People get sick, sometimes several at the same time if it's flu season. We once had two staff members at once with broken ankles! Cross-training staff is a good idea for emergency coverage. It's also great for "walking in someone else's shoes"; it helps build morale by allowing staff members to empathize with one another.

- *Free training by other departments or agencies.* Look around to see if other departments or agencies offer training that would be relevant for you and your staff. The risk-management department might offer tapes or even presentations on the proper way to lift heavy items (think about how much a stack of books weighs!). Your automation department might offer a presentation on the care and feeding of your computers, thus preventing such disasters as a clean-freak staff member spraying the screen full blast with window cleaner. A nearby library may be conducting training on the same software your library uses. The fire department will be glad to talk on such things as how to evacuate a building full of people when there's an emergency. These emergencies do happen: Fumes from a cleaning solvent can get into your air intake system; a severe storm can make your roof collapse; an overloaded electrical outlet can start a fire. (We used to have a photocopier that routinely overheated, catching the paper on fire and sending out bright orange flames. It took years to get budget approval to replace it!) Proper training and procedures need to be in place to prevent injury or even death.

Sometimes, discipline problems can be the result of too little or no training. With improper training, it's possible for a person to make the same mistake over and over and over. In one instance, when the magnetic security strips for library materials first came on the scene, a brand-new employee was given the task of checking in books. This included running the books over a magnetic station, resensitizing the strips. She was very quick and efficient, and in no time flat, she had gone through the cart of paperbacks and made a considerable dent in the stack of books on tape. Her supervisor had forgotten to tell this person that when you get a book on tape near a magnet, it's erased. The library lost hundreds of dollars' worth of audiobooks, and the new staff member felt terrible (she was afraid she'd be fired). The supervisor learned the hard way that you need a checklist of training items and that once those are covered, you stay by the new employee (or assign an experienced staff member to monitor that person) until proficiency and understanding are shown on each task.

FIRING AND OTHER CORRECTIVE ACTIONS

Yes, you will have staff you want to fire. (You'll even have staff you want to smack!) No matter how well you manage or supervise, face it, there are always slackers and people with bad attitudes. However, you can't just point your finger at someone and say, "You're fired!" (And you're not allowed to smack 'em!)

Personnel law generally requires that some sort of progressive discipline precede terminating an employee. This assumes that the person whose performance isn't up to par refuses to change his or her ways. Steps of progressive discipline may include the following:

- Counseling the employee about their poor performance or behavior and verbalizing your expectations. Be specific and direct. Don't beat around the bush. Stay calm and on point.
- Giving the employee a written warning in the form of a memo or letter of expectations in which you state that his or her behavior or performance is unacceptable and you expect it to change. Sometimes, this is the only written notice.
- Counseling the employee a second time.
- Giving the employee a formal letter of reprimand. Written disciplinary notices to employees should include the reason for the disciplinary action; the corrective action that will take place; the effective date(s); and the employee's right to respond orally or in writing and the time frame for doing so.
- Giving the employee a notice of intent to suspend.
- Placing the employee on suspension (can be with or without pay).
- Giving the employee a notice of intent to terminate.
- Terminating the employee.

Also, administrative leave, sometimes called investigative leave, is available. This requires the employee in question to stay away from the work site until the investigation is complete. This sort of leave can take place with or without notice, can be paid or unpaid, and doesn't require progressive discipline. Administrative leaves are put into effect when an employee steals or misappropriates public property, fights or displays other outbursts of violent behavior on the job, endangers others, or shows open and blatant insubordination (although this one is a tricky thing to prove). The employee is informed in writing about the dates the administrative leave will take place and the status of his pay while on leave.

Many organizations hire staff on a probationary basis. The person is on probation for a period that typically ranges from three months to a year. During that time, the new hire can be terminated without the benefit of all the steps of progressive disciple. However, there still needs to be a reason to dismiss and documentation to back it up, and it should be done in conjunction with your organization's human resources department. In an "at will" state, an employee may be dismissed at any time for any reason or for no reason at all. In these states, it is usually to your advantage not to list a cause for dismissal, because it can't be contested legally if no cause is given. Make sure you know which type of state you're in and the applicable laws.

Part-time, contractual, substitute, floater, and temporary employees can usually be terminated at the director's discretion. Once more, make sure there's a reason to terminate, and document your action.

Find out what your organization's progressive disciplinary actions are and follow them to a T. *Never* do a formal disciplinary action without running it past your supervisor and your human resources department. *Never* do a formal disciplinary action without comprehensive back-up documentation. *Always* document disciplinary actions and the reasons for them. Include such details as dates and times.

Don't knee-jerk when you consider disciplinary actions. If you're angry, cool down before you speak to the employee. If two employees are having a disagreement, don't assume the one who comes to you first is the one in the right. Listen to both sides. Try very hard not to play favorites.

Never rebuke or discipline an employee in front of other people. A simple "May I see you in my office for a moment?" is far more professional and less demeaning than a public admonishment. Always treat people the way you'd like to be treated.

Before taking corrective action against an employee, be aware of personal needs that sometimes affect performance. These can include such things as transportation difficulties, medical needs, and care problems for children or elderly parents. Try working with the employee to come to a mutually agreeable solution before beginning any disciplinary action.

A high turnover rate is a sign of poor management, whether it's due to terminations or resignations. Don't take firing an employee lightly. Remember that employees are people first. By terminating someone, you are, quite possibly, taking away income that would pay for the family's living expenses, including food, electricity, and housing. However, by ignoring the behavior of an employee sorely in need of termination, you ruin the morale of the rest of your staff, and if that employee's actions are odious enough, you have set the stage for a hostile work environment.

LAYOFFS

Laying off an employee can be harder than terminating one for disciplinary reasons, because both you and that person know that he or she did absolutely nothing to deserve being separated from your place of employment. Layoffs can be for various reasons They range from a temporary layoff to the more permanent reduction in force (RIF). Layoffs are often the result of budgetary problems. In many cases, layoffs begin with temporary staff. Regular staff are usually laid off according to seniority. In any case, layoffs have a terrible effect on employee morale and can even lead to so-called survivor's guilt.

IN SUMMARY

When hiring, disciplining, laying off, or firing employees, legal and ethical considerations come into play. You need to know policies, rules, regulations, and laws that affect these actions. Be sure your staff is aware of these, too. Make it a point to learn these policies and rules yourself, and then follow them to the letter when the need arises. Always be fair to everyone involved.

CHAPTER 6

Friends and Volunteers

Nobody can do everything, but everyone can do something.
—Author unknown

We are not alone. And it's a good thing! Though some cynics have accused Friends and volunteers of living on another planet, they are valuable players on a library's team. While those who don't work in libraries may have a viewpoint that's very different from those who do, they can make many important contributions. Few libraries have all the staff they need. Judicious use of Friends and volunteers can permit libraries to perform many tasks that might not otherwise get done.

FRIENDS OF THE LIBRARY

Begin by doing your research. If you don't already know, find out whether your library has a Friends of the Library group. Find out what documentation regarding the group already exists. How, when, why was it established? Does it have bylaws? Discover the history of the group. Learn what the status of the group is today. Is it active? Is it on the back burner and in need of reactivation? Is there a slate of officers? Does it have a set of bylaws or other guidelines? Or do they need to be developed?

At a minimum, a Friends group should have a mission statement and a set of bylaws. A list of goals or activities is also useful to have. Some degree of formality is needed to keep things copacetic.

ASSISTANCE FOR YOUR FRIENDS GROUP

Whether trying to form a new group or reactivate an old one, a resource that can prove invaluable is Friends of Libraries U.S.A. (FOLUSA).

FOLUSA's mission is to "motivate and support state and local library support groups across the country in their efforts to preserve and strengthen libraries, and to create awareness and appreciation of library services."[1] FOLUSA can help with the establishment of a new Friends group or the development of an existing one. FOLUSA also works with library boards and provides assistance in promoting the library.

FOLUSA offers various types of memberships. An individual interested in library issues on the national level can establish a personal membership. Personal members receive FOLUSA's bimonthly newsletter and can receive FOLUSA's toolkit, *Starting a New Friends Group, or Revitalizing the Group You Have,* and a sample operating agreement between a library and a Friends group. A local Friends group or a library can join FOLUSA and receive a great deal of valuable assistance with their local group. And businesses can become FOLUSA members and thereby show their support for libraries. Complete membership information is available on the membership page at www.folusa.org/membership.

FOLUSA can be contacted by phone at (215) 790-1674, or toll free at (800) 9FOLUSA. They can be reached via e-mail at friends@ folusa.org or through their Web site at www.folusa.org.

BOOK SALES

An ever-popular fund-raiser for libraries is the book sale, often conducted by the Friends of the Library group. The items sold at these sales (often more than just books) generally come from one of two sources: (1) materials donated to the library that are not useful additions to the collection or (2) materials withdrawn from the library's collection because they are no longer useful.

In some localities, librarians have run into conflict with state or local property laws, which restrict what can be done with library property. Often, these laws state that library property (including ex-property, such as withdrawn materials) cannot be lent, sold, or given away. In other words, no-longer-useful materials can legally be put in the dumpster or burned, but they cannot be sold to generate revenue for the purchase of new library materials or traded for something useful.

Some librarians have been able to work around this counterproductive situation. In some areas, the law states that the library board can adopt a policy regarding the disposition of library materials. What these libraries have done is help their board develop a policy stating that all nonmonetary donations to the library become the property of the Friends of the Library group and, likewise, that all materials withdrawn from the library become the property of the Friends group. Furthermore, the policy specifies that the Friends group may dispose of such property as it sees fit.

The Friends group, in turn, develops a policy that says the library gets first pick of all materials donated to it and empowers the library staff charged with developing the collection to be the voice of the library in deciding which materials to keep for the library and which to discard. Any materials chosen by the staff are given to the library by the Friends and are added to the collection; any materials not so chosen remain the property of the Friends. The Friends group, then, determines how to dispose of the remaining materials. Some may be deemed unsuitable for sale and trashed. Others may be exchanged with other libraries for items of interest to the local library via a duplicates exchange program such as the Duplicates Exchange Union of the American Library Association.[2]

Likewise, materials discarded from the library become the property of the Friends group. With guidance from the library staff, the Friends group decides which materials are to be sold, which should be trashed, and which may be exchanged with other libraries.

THE FRIENDS BOOK SALE

The many ways to organize a book sale fall basically into two types: (1) an occasional book sale or (2) a perpetual book sale.

The occasional book sale is held at some specific point in time, perhaps annually or semiannually, depending on how fast materials accumulate and how much assistance can be rallied to conduct the sale. The Friends group publicizes, organizes, and conducts the sale and collects the funds received from it.

The perpetual book sale is held on an ongoing basis. It may be something as simple as a table full of materials on display in the library. Library patrons can peruse the materials, pick out those they want, and pay for them at the circulation desk. Bear in mind that it may be important legally for there to be a clear understanding that the circulation desk is simply collecting those funds on behalf of the Friends group; there needs to be a clear accounting of those funds and a formal transfer of those funds to the Friends.

Some libraries, particularly those that are able to collect a larger amount of materials, may have a used bookstore (again, including much more than just books) within the library. A specialized room or two dedicated to this purpose and placed under the purview of the Friends is a feature we are seeing built into many new library buildings. All potential sale materials are placed in one of these rooms and, after proper processing, are either given to the library for addition to the collection or moved to a publicly accessible room designated as the bookstore. The store may be open whenever the library is, or, more likely, just a few hours a week, whenever the Friends group is able to find volunteers to staff it. Such bookstores are often wildly popular with patrons, generating much goodwill and often resulting in more donations.

It is vitally important that some kind of understanding be reached *in advance* as to how and when funds will be funneled back into the library. Far too often, Friends groups have used such funds to purchase something for the library that was not needed, or, at least, was not top priority for the library.

GIFT STORE

Extending the idea of the bookstore a bit further, or perhaps in lieu thereof, you might wish to have a library gift store. Myriad items can stock such a store, such as pens, pencils, notepads, mouse pads, coffee mugs, book bags, aprons, and bookmarks—all bearing the library logo, of course. The Friends group can take charge of designing and stocking such items, working with the library staff for the sale thereof. The sale of these items might be through the bookstore, through a separate gift store, or if your library isn't large enough to support such an arrangement, just by offering the items for sale through the circulation desk. As with items from the book sale, a policy for distributing those funds to the library needs to be clearly established beforehand.

VOLUNTEERS

The most important consideration in using volunteers is to have a plan. Libraries that have allowed volunteers to randomly wander in and out have often soon found themselves in the middle of a problem that's difficult to solve. A formal structure in which the volunteers can function is essential.

First of all, volunteers need to be screened. You must make sure that the interests and abilities of volunteers match the needs of the library. As director, you must make sure that someone is in charge of your volunteer program. It may fall to you as director, or a specific staff member may be charged with the task. You might even consider using a reliable and experienced volunteer to oversee your volunteer program.

After designating the point person for the volunteers, a good starting place in founding a viable volunteer program is to create a list of possible duties. When a volunteer approaches the library asking, "What can I do?" be prepared to present that person with a list of tasks that need doing. The reality of a list of bona fide tasks may focus the over-enthusiastic but ill-equipped volunteer.

Many types of jobs in a library can be performed quite competently by a volunteer. The exact list of jobs will vary based on the library, so no list can be exhaustive, but here are some suggestions:

- *Mending books and other materials.* Libraries always have materials that need repair. Those who are dexterous can devote themselves to the repair of such items, while a less nimble-fingered volunteer might be used to search the stacks to find materials in need of repair. Be sure you have the proper supplies to mend library materials so these volunteers have the resources they need to perform this task.
- *Label typing.* If your library still uses typed labels, a good typist can offer major assistance in this area. It must be emphasized, however, that if the typing involves call numbers or other identification data, 100 percent accuracy is imperative.

- *Cleaning.* Libraries always need cleaning, whether it's the cleaning of books and other materials or the dusting of shelves, display areas, and so forth. But before assigning volunteers to clean, make sure they're willing to do that type of work and that there are no counterindicative health issues, such as allergies or asthma.

- *Inventorying.* Because this is a job that libraries often lack time to do, volunteers can provide invaluable assistance in making it happen. Bear in mind, however, that inventorying is an exact science and should only be assigned to someone who's good at keeping accurate records. Also remember that extensive training may be necessary before someone is ready to tackle inventory. Do you have a staff member prepared to train the volunteer?

- *Greeting/staffing a help desk.* Some libraries use volunteers to give people a friendly greeting at the door and ask how they may be of service. Such volunteers may be trained to answer simple queries, such as directional questions. In a more formal setting, some volunteers may staff a help desk.

- *Bookselling.* Libraries that have some kind of book sale may use a volunteer to staff that area and collect funds. Needless to say, because that person will be handling funds, such a volunteer should be someone whose honesty is beyond question.

- *Answering the phone.* A volunteer might be used to answer incoming calls and direct them to the correct area of the library. Some training will likely be necessary so the volunteer is able to distinguish, for example, a circulation call from a reference question.

- *Shelving.* Shelving, of course, is one of those jobs that require a high rate of accuracy. The library needs to develop some type of skill test, such as the traditional sorting of index cards with call numbers on them, before simply assigning a volunteer to shelve. Don't send volunteers into the stacks alone to shelve until you are absolutely certain of their accuracy. In addition to placing items in the proper place, a trained and skillful volunteer can read and straighten shelves.

- *Photocopying and filing.* A volunteer might render office-type services by assisting with some of the paperwork. Or this person might staff the public photocopying area to offer assistance with the machines, whether it be adding paper or toner or showing the public how to use them.

- *Entering data.* A volunteer with good data-entry skills can help create and maintain a library database, such as the online catalog or other types of library files. We cannot, however, overemphasize the importance of keeping the data "clean." This would be the *last* job we'd assign someone we couldn't depend on for 100 percent accuracy. It's better that the data go unentered than that it be entered with errors.

- *Processing materials.* Getting items ready for circulation requires a lot of steps: affixing labels, attaching plastic covers, perhaps inserting cards and pockets, and so forth. A volunteer might be trained in a single step or in the series of steps necessary to get an item shelf ready.

- *Delivering materials to the homebound.* Because some volunteers, particularly senior citizens, may be social creatures who really enjoy human interaction, this may be an excellent use of volunteer time. However, there may be significant liabilities. Check with library legal counsel on the risks and liabilities of having volunteers traveling in their own vehicles (or the library's) and on the risks of sending a volunteer into someone's home. It may be complex. In any case, the ground rules need to be clear so that the job is done efficiently and effectively. For example, you don't want a volunteer who spends hours with one person while shortchanging the others. It needs to be clearly spelled out which types of social interaction are permissible and which are not.

- *Preparing display materials.* Some volunteers may have great artistic abilities and be experts in preparing bulletin boards or other types of displays. Having a good, detailed volunteer application form can help reveal talent of this type that might otherwise go unnoticed.

- *Preparing publicity.* Likewise, some volunteers may have talent and experience in preparing marketing materials or those that describe a specific library service, such as your outstanding genealogy collection. Perhaps someone may be proficient in designing a library newsletter. This is the type of expertise you don't want to overlook.

- *Helping with the children.* Volunteers who have good rapport with children might help out in the children's room or during special events such as story hour. Due to the inherent risks of authorizing a volunteer to work around children, be sure to predetermine with legal counsel what is prudent. Anyone who works with children should pass a police background check first.

- *Running AV equipment.* If volunteers have experience with the operation or maintenance of audiovisual equipment, they can help out at movie times or during speaker programs when such equipment is used. A volunteer can also help you set up seats and tables and take them down when a program is over.

- *Helping with the computers.* If you are fortunate enough to get volunteers who are computer fluent, they might be interested in providing a helping hand to patrons with their computer activities. A carefully screened, well-trained volunteer can assist in the computer area. Clear rules must be laid out, such as "Don't touch the patron's personal computer for any reason!" if that's the library policy. Should a volunteer be accused (correctly or erroneously) of damaging someone's computer or losing important files, the library could face big problems.

- *Giving tours.* Perhaps you have a historical or otherwise noteworthy building or collection, such as a local history collection. A properly trained volunteer can serve as a docent to give tours of the building or the special area.

- *Assisting circulation-desk staff.* A volunteer with good public-service skills might assist the staff at the circulation desk. Others might help behind the scenes in a nonpublic area by performing tasks such as checking in or presorting materials for reshelving. It's important to remember that patron records are confidential and must be treated as such.

- *Assisting with interlibrary loan.* A properly trained volunteer can help verify citation information, pull needed items from the shelf or confirm their circulation status, or help package items for shipping. A volunteer could call patrons to notify them that their requested loan item has arrived and is available for use.

- *Working on special projects.* These, of course, will vary by library. Some volunteers, particularly those who have been around for a while, may even have ideas of their own for special projects that the library hasn't yet considered.

- *Providing their point of view.* This is not a specific task, but keep in mind that many library volunteers are there because they are library users. One of the ways they can assist you is by providing a patron's viewpoint on whatever topic or situation is at hand.

BRINGING A VOLUNTEER ON BOARD

Step 1: The Application Process

Make sure that the volunteer process is formalized. Any volunteer approaching the library should first be handed an application form. This may or may not be the same application form used for employees. Check with the library's legal counsel for their recommendation. A good application form will help the library discover the talents of the volunteers and assign volunteers to the appropriate tasks.

Step 2: The Interview

Conduct an interview, just as you would with a prospective employee. The air of formality that this step lends to the process is likely to help volunteers take their jobs more seriously. This type of formality can also help should it ever become necessary to discharge a volunteer. But primarily, a formal (or quasi-formal) interview will allow you to best match the volunteer to an area of service needing particular talents or abilities. It will also provide a greater likelihood that everyone is happy with the assignment.

Step 3: Job Assignments

Assign a job (or jobs) and establish a schedule. Asking volunteers just to show up whenever they feel like it to do whatever job may need doing at the time is simply asking for problems, not the least of which is that the volunteer may become bored and quit coming at all.

While volunteers have a great deal of say-so in setting their schedules, they need to understand that the library expects them to show up as promised and to perform the agreed-upon tasks. Volunteers are expected to *work* during their volunteer time and to stay on task.

Be sure your volunteers have a safe place to put their possessions (such as purses) during their work shift, perhaps a locker or a lockable desk drawer. Also, many libraries give their volunteers name badges so staff and the public can identify them.

Step 4: Orientation and Training

Once a volunteer has been "contracted," it's time for orientation and training. It needs to be clearly established who will train the volunteer and when, and how much time will be devoted to training. You don't want to reach the point of diminishing returns: when it takes longer to train a volunteer to do the job than for someone on staff to do it.

The library should have a volunteer manual, containing the rules, regulations, and procedures that volunteers are expected to follow. During the orientation phase, volunteers should be given time to read and learn the manual, and it should be made clear that they are responsible for knowing its contents. In those cases where it's desirable or necessary, develop some sort of follow-up activity to test their knowledge.

The manual might also contain "how-to" information for performing those tasks that are frequently undertaken by volunteers, particularly those tasks that are frequently performed by multiple people. The procedures might be part of the same manual or be contained in separate documents perhaps separated by department: Circulation would have its own procedures manual, Technical Services would have its own, and so on.

Whatever you do, don't waste time reinventing the wheel. The Web is replete with examples of volunteer manuals. Or you might ask other librarians with whom you have a good working relationship if you can borrow theirs for a starter.

If volunteers serve a lengthy shift, such as a half or full day, it needs to be established that they are entitled to a regular break. It also needs to be clear whether volunteers are welcome to use the staff break room, restrooms, or other staff facilities. If coffee or donuts or other snacks are provided to staff, make it clear to volunteers whether they are welcome to partake and on what basis. If staff members make contributions for their coffee, let volunteers know whether they need to do their part. On the other hand, a cup of coffee and a donut or muffin can go a long way toward making volunteers feel appreciated and welcome.

Some libraries schedule a regular volunteer day (weekly, monthly, or at some other predetermined time) when all volunteers show up to work at the same time. It's certainly great if the library provides refreshments for such times. Sometimes, regular staff are willing to take turns providing them, or even the volunteers might want to take a turn.

Step 5: Evaluation

While a formal evaluation process, such as with staff, may not be necessary, someone *must* supervise and evaluate the volunteers' work. How formal the process needs to be will depend on your library and the nature of your volunteers. But, at the very least, a good volunteer should be receiving frequent encouragement for a job well done.

Unfortunately, some volunteers may become disruptive, wasting not only their own time but getting in the way and wasting staff time as well. Perhaps they're just chatty, or lonely and in need of conversation, but it can cause problems. You need to be prepared with some kind of behavior code for volunteers. In some cases, a simple reassignment may be all that is necessary.

Unfortunately, not every volunteer works out. Be prepared to deal with it. Make sure there is a clear policy regarding dismissal. Some volunteers may end up doing more socializing than work. Others may have overstated or misstated their abilities. Some, it may be discovered, have substance-abuse or mental or emotional problems that result in behavior which cannot be condoned. And, unfortunately, an occasional volunteer may turn out to be just plain dishonest. The same rules of behavior that apply to staff must be applied to volunteers.

Dismissing a volunteer is neither an easy nor a pleasant task, but it can be an unfortunate reality. Being prepared beforehand is the best tool. The advice of legal counsel in such preparation is, of course, the best defense.

Be sure to keep records of your volunteers' activities, such as a logbook of arrivals and departures. Clear, concise logs can often serve a purpose far beyond that for which they were intended. For example, showing how many hours of volunteer time during the year were necessary to keep the library running can go a long way toward showing the library board how desperately new staff positions are needed. In any case, accurate record keeping can be useful at the year's end for awarding volunteers the recognition they so richly deserve. And, if necessary, an accurate record of no-shows can be useful in dismissing a volunteer, should that become necessary.

Step 6: Reward Them!

Everyone likes to be recognized for a job well done. In addition to frequent "thank-yous," find some formal or semiformal way of giving your volunteers the recognition they deserve. Some libraries have an annual breakfast, lunch, or dinner, sometimes in connection with the Christmas holiday, sometimes near the end of the school year before people tend to disappear for the summer. Sometimes the library staff hosts a pitch-in or potluck for the volunteers. Sometimes book-sale money can be set aside for a volunteer appreciation activity.

Everyone likes to receive recognition. Give the volunteers some type of certificate; these can be purchased or easily generated on the library's computer. Some libraries give volunteers an annual pin, for one year, two years, five years, or ten years of service. These can be found at a business-supply, school-supply, sports-supply or church-supply store or online.

At the breakfast, lunch, or dinner, recognize each volunteer individually. Have each one come down front, or at least stand, to receive his or her certificate. Give a brief summary of the volunteer's accomplishments during the year. If Sam has mended 300 books and Maria has created a new brochure for the library, say so!

Keep your volunteers active, keep them interested, afford them as much gratitude and recognition as you possibly can, and you'll never lack for volunteers.

The Legalities

Before accepting your first volunteer, you need to talk extensively with the library legal counsel to see what the risks and obligations for the library are. What is the liability to the library if a volunteer is hurt on the job? Is the volunteer covered by the library's insurance? *Can* volunteers be covered by library insurance for an additional premium and is it worth the expense? How does the library's workers' compensation program regard volunteers? You need to be very clear on the legalities of using volunteers before starting any kind of volunteer program. Even if a volunteer program has been in existence since before you became director, you need to make very sure you are clear on all the liabilities and obligations.

FINDING VOLUNTEERS

How do you go about finding volunteers? Sometimes, they appear as if by magic: Library patrons may simply decide they'd like to devote some time to the library and they just "up and offer." But what if your library needs help and the volunteers don't magically appear?

The Friends of the Library group may be a good source of volunteers. They may have a formalized volunteer program in place, or they may just be a source of "warm bodies." If people are members of the Friends, they obviously are library supporters and may be disposed to help if only someone would ask. Whatever the case, don't overlook this potentially rich source of volunteers.

Additionally, search your community for volunteers. Try contacting social-service organizations.

Many communities have local service organizations such as the Retired Senior Volunteer Program (RSVP), which has members from all walks of life. Some are retired professionals whose expertise may be a valuable asset in helping with such areas as the library's finances. These seniors volunteer their time through RSVP, and the agency assigns them to different tasks throughout the community. Give the agency a call and let them know the needs of the library in terms of numbers, time, and types of tasks.

COMMUNITY SERVICE

Sometimes people are sentenced by the courts to perform local community service because of some minor offense. The library can be a beneficiary of such service. By working with the judicial system, you can find out if some of these people might make a good volunteer for the library. In many cases, the nature of their offense would in no way impede the quality of their service. Work through your local legal authorities to establish a list of offenses that might provide acceptable volunteers and those that would not. You wouldn't want someone accused of theft, for example, to be working with money. People convicted of violent, drug-related, or sexual offenses should not be considered for your community-service program. Make sure that, in any given instance, the library has the right of refusal.

Another source of community-service volunteers is your local high school or community college. Some schools have school-to-work vocational programs in which students receive school credit for performing a given number of hours of community service. Others may have some type of vocational exploration program in which students go out into the workaday world and spend time in different work environments. Contact one of the counselors at your local school to find out if such programs exist in your area.

INTERNS

If your community is near a library school, there may be those working on their library degree who need some experience to build up their résumé. Contact the library school and let them know of opportunities for interns in your library. Even if a school is not all that near, there may be students who are home for the summer, on weekends, or between semesters who would be glad to volunteer some of their time in exchange for the experience. In this day and age, there might even be library science students who live near the library but attend classes online and need to gain practical experience in a library near their home.

IN SUMMARY

Everybody needs friends. And every library we've ever seen needs more staff. Judicious use of Friends and volunteers will allow the library to reach levels of public service and goodwill otherwise unattainable. Such relationships need to be formalized to avoid potential problems, and the library needs to explore the legal implications before starting either a volunteer program or a Friends of the Library group.

NOTES

1. www.folusa.org/about/who-we-are.php. Accessed August 21, 2007.
2. www.ala.org/ala/alcts/alctspubs/duplicatesexch/duplicatesexchange. htm. Accessed August 21, 2007.

CHAPTER 7

"Managing" the Board: Who They Are, and How to Build and Maintain Consensus—A Tricky Tightrope

The speed of the boss is the speed of the team.
—Lee Iacocca, American business leader

WHO'S YOUR BOSS?

As library director, you might report directly to a state or county librarian, city or town manager, another department head in your organization (for instance, when parks, recreation, and library are combined into one division), or the mayor and council. No matter what your chain of command, your library will probably have a library board or board of trustees. You will either answer to this board or be advised by them. At any rate, it's imperative that you be familiar with your board and their legal authority and responsibilities.

Library boards are usually one of two types, administrative (sometimes called governing) or advisory. Both are made up of elected members, political appointees, or a combination of the two. Library boards are typically established and controlled by public ordinance, and they operate under strict rules and bylaws:

- Legal authority—the statute under which established
- Library Board

  - Number of members
  - Whether members are elected or appointed
  - Length of a member's term
  - Date on which members' terms begin
  - Policy regarding consecutive terms
  - Powers and duties of board members

- Officers

  - Who the officers are (president, secretary, treasurer)
  - Method of selecting officers
  - Powers and duties of each office

- Board meetings

  - Meeting dates
  - Meeting place
  - Agenda
  - Order of business
  - Reference to compliance to Open Meetings Act
  - Availability of accommodations for people with disabilities

- Committees

  - Standing committees
  - Additional committees

- Amending the bylaws (usually a two-thirds vote)[1]

The number of board members varies from area to area. Usually, there are an odd number of members in order to avoid a tied vote. Lengths of term vary, and terms may be staggered. U.S. citizenship may be a requirement. Residency in that town or county is a typical requirement for membership on a library board. Members might be required to be qualified electors (18 years of age and older), but some towns and cities have younger teen board members to represent their youth constituents. The Glendale (Arizona) Advisory Library Board, for example, "advises the City Council on policies related to the administration and provision of library services." The Board has nine members appointed by the city council for two-year terms, among which are two high school students.[2] (In most cases, when libraries have a teen advisory board, it is a separate board and is advisory only in nature.)

Sometimes, a financial disclosure statement is required before a person can be appointed to the library board. Board members are usually forbidden to hold a paid office or have employment in the government entity during their tenure on the board. Although it's not a common practice, some boards, such as the Minneapolis Public Library Board of Trustees, are compensated for their service, with general members earning $600 each month, and the president $700.[3]

ADMINISTRATIVE, OR GOVERNING, LIBRARY BOARDS

If your library has an administrative library board, you will most likely report directly to it. This type of board can have the ability to hire and fire you and to control the library budget and have final say as to how it can be spent. Also known as governing boards, administrative library boards are legally responsible for the library and everything that happens in it.

In Plant City, Florida, a commission appoints a seven-member administrative board that "establishes rules and regulations for the library, subject to the supervision and control of the city commission." In addition, the board has "exclusive control of expenditures of all monies donated on behalf of the library."[4]

Pocahontas, Iowa, has an administrative library board. They have identified the five primary roles of their board:

- "Advocate for the library in the community and advocate for the community as a member of the library board."
- "Plan for the future of the library."
- "Monitor and evaluate the overall effectiveness of the library."
- "Set library policies."
- "Hire and evaluate the library director."[5]

The Monona (Wisconsin) Library Board is administrative and "semi-autonomous." They are empowered by Wisconsin state law as well as Monona city ordinance "to act as the governing body" of the library, and are considered an "arm" of city government. Their legal responsibilities are listed as follows:

- "Determining the goals and objectives of the Library in order to plan and carry out library services"

- "Determining and adopting written policies to govern all aspects of the operation of the Library"
- "Preparing an annual budget and having exclusive control of all monies appropriated by the City Council or given to the library through gifts, bequests, contracts, grants or awards"
- "Employing a competent staff to administer its policies and carry out its programs."[6]

In Enid, Oklahoma, the library board is administrative. They have the "exclusive control of the expenditure of all moneys collected and placed to the credit of the Library Fund, of the construction of any library building, and of the supervision, care and custody of the grounds, rooms, or buildings constructed, leased or set apart for that purpose." The board also has the power to do the following:

- "Lease and obtain rooms for the use of said library."
- "Appoint a suitable Librarian and necessary assistants and fix their compensation, and…remove such appointees."
- "Purchase ground and erect thereon a suitable building for the use of said library, and…, with the approval of the City Commission,…sell and dispose of any property acquired by purchase, or by other means when the Board by proper resolution finds that said property is not needed for library purposes."
- Accept, or in its discretion…decline donations, and for the purpose of maintaining and augmenting collections other than collections of printed books and periodicals, may, in its discretion, expend moneys or incur obligations not exceeding in any one year, ten per cent of the whole amount paid into the Library Fund for such a year."[7]

ADVISORY LIBRARY BOARDS

It's easy to see the difference between administrative (governing) and advisory library boards in these lists developed by the Library of Virginia. In that state, library boards are given specific lists of their rules, duties, and responsibilities. Governing or administrative boards have these authorities, roles, and duties:

- "Employ a competent and qualified library director; maintain an ongoing performance appraisal process for the director."

- "Determine the mission and goals and objectives of the library, and adopt written policies governing the library."
- "Secure adequate funds to carry out the library's program; assist in the preparation of the annual budget. Officially approve budget requests."
- "Ensure that the library has a long-range planning process that considers the library's strengths and weaknesses, and can be implemented and evaluated."
- "Be familiar with local, state, and federal library laws; actively support pending library legislation."
- "Establish, support, and participate in a planned public relations program."
- "Attend all board meetings and see that accurate records are kept on file at the library."
- "Attend regional, state, and national trustee meetings and workshops."
- "Know the services of the Library of Virginia."
- "Report regularly to the governing officials and the general public."[8]

Advisory library board members in Virginia, on the other hand, are given these authority, roles, and duties:

- "Recommend a competent and qualified library director."
- "Consider and recommend written policies governing the library."
- "Participate in efforts to secure adequate funds to carry out the library's program."
- "Assist in a long-range planning process that considers the library's strengths and weaknesses, and can be implemented and evaluated."
- "Be familiar with local, state, and federal laws; actively support pending library legislation."
- "Establish, support, and participate in a planned public relations program."
- "Attend all board meetings and see that accurate records are kept on file at the library."
- "Attend regional, state, and national trustee meetings and workshops."
- "Know the services of the Library of Virginia."
- "Report regularly to the governing officials and the general public."

Advisory library boards, just as the name indicates, serve in an advisory capacity to both the library director and the city council. This is the case with the Longmont, Colorado, Library Board, which is charged with the following functions:

- "Prepare a long-range plan for library services;
- Review the Library's annual budget request;
- Consider all policy matters pertaining to the Public Library and make recommendations to the City Council;
- Advise City Council as to the expenditure of funds or securities devised or given to the Board for library purposes; and
- Prepare an annual written report to the City Council showing the condition of the trust and the operations of the Public Library."[9]

Notice the verbs that describe the board's function: *review, consider, prepare,* and *advise.* The board plays an important role and is expected to "provide guidance to the City Council in directing the activities and goals of library operations." In Longmont, the library director serves as an ex officio (nonvoting) member of the board.

In Ferndale, Michigan, the library director is also an ex officio member of the board. The Ferndale Library Board is responsible for "the operation of the public library, adopting long- and short-range plans for the library's growth, deciding on the course of action and setting schedules for implementing plans, and serving as the 'connecting link' between the library and the community."[10] Although not always written, the idea of the library board as a "connecting link" between the library and the community is a reality. Members of library boards are typically well connected politically, and can be your best ally . . . or your worst enemy.

Santa Barbara, California, has an advisory library board. This board is required to do the following:

- "Make recommendations to the City Council concerning the operation and conduct of the City library facilities for which the City is responsible.
- Recommend to the City Council rules, regulations and by-laws for the administration and protection of the facilities.
- Recommend to the City Council the duties and qualifications of the Library Director.
- Recommend policies concerning acquisition, disposition, availability, and use of publications and other property.
- Consider, with the Library Director, the annual Library budget and make recommendations to the City Council and City Administrator.
- Report to the City Council, within 60 days after the close of the fiscal year, on the work, accomplishments, and conditions of the libraries during the preceding fiscal year."[11]

On the other hand, some libraries, such as the Franklin, Massachusetts, Public Library, the oldest library in the United States, have a simple statement about the role of the library board: "The Franklin Library Board of Directors is appointed by the town administrator of the town of Franklin and accepted by the town council. The board acts in an advisory capacity to the library director and the town administrator."[12] A broad statement such as this can give the board and library director lots of latitude within which to develop their respective roles.

Board authority and power are always on a continuum, whether the board is advisory or administrative, and finding the balance between their role and yours, as director, can sometimes prove to be a tricky feat. As you search for that balance, try to remember that the board can be your best ally...or your worst enemy.

THE SHARED GOAL: THE BEST SERVICE POSSIBLE FOR YOUR PUBLIC

Board members are invaluable in providing advocacy, soliciting community involvement, and providing positive public relations. In the city of Scottsdale, Arizona, the library board is advisory. The board "advises the City Council on general policy relating to the programs, services and future development of the Scottsdale Public Library."[13] This board has another function: overseeing the Library Trust Fund. Money that is generated through the sale of used books and magazines goes into this trust fund, which is used to purchase much-needed library materials.

A TYPICAL BOARD MEETING

Your library board needs to be kept in the loop of what's happening within the library. No one likes to be blindsided, and the members of your board are no exception. It's a good idea to meet at least once a month. If your board is meeting less frequently and you have some leeway to suggest more frequent meetings, you might consider doing so, though the intervals of meetings are usually determined by ordinance or bylaws.

Due to the Open Meetings Act (Public Law 94–409), which passed at the federal level in 1977 as part of the "government-in-the-sunshine" law, such actions as announcing a meeting at least a week in advance and posting the agenda (date, time, and location) before the meeting are mandatory. Requirements vary from state to state, so check with your organization's attorney for your state's specific requirements. The Open Meetings Act has very few exceptions other than for such things as discussion of a personnel issue. Only under specific circumstances can the meeting be closed.

A typical agenda might include the following:

- Call to order
- Roll call
- Approval of the agenda
- Approval of the minutes of the previous meeting
- Treasurer's report
- Committee reports
- Director's report
- Old business
- New business
- Public comment
- Adjournment
- Additional notices

    - Reference to compliance to Open Meetings Act
    - Availability of accommodations for people with disabilities

No one likes to be at a dull meeting, so when it comes time for your report to the board, think of ways to make it interesting. For example, your part of the meeting might include a report from a staff member about a special project or program. Make sure that each board member gets copies of your library handouts, such as summer reading club bookmarks, bibliographies, or program information. If you can, prepare a packet for each board member and deliver it in advance. Don't forget to serve refreshments!

KEEPING RELATIONS FRIENDLY!

Be friendly. Greet each board member personally at every meeting. They're volunteering their precious time, so make them feel welcome. Verbalize your appreciation.

Don't play favorites. Most boards will have their share of warm, fuzzy, upbeat members and cranky, negative, unfriendly members. It's so easy to gravitate toward the likeable members, but every member needs to feel needed and appreciated, and no one likes a library director's "pet." Remember: Never, never gossip about a board member with another board member.

Try to remain politically neutral. Your board members are somehow connected to your political leaders. You don't want to be identified with one side or another.

Establish and maintain open communications. Be open and honest. Listen to board members' ideas and suggestions, even if the board isn't administrative.

Be willing to compromise. You might have one idea of how things should go, and the board might have another. Try to find a middle ground and build consensus.

IN SUMMARY

Library boards are either *administrative,* which basically means they're in charge of everything, including you, or *advisory,* which means they offer advice and serve as a conduit between you, your elected officials, and the community. Whether your library has an administrative or advisory library board, good relations are a must. This comes from friendliness, good communications, and the willingness to compromise. It all sounds so easy, but like every other relationship in your life, the one with your library board takes lots of time and effort to keep it healthy.

NOTES

1. Ellen Richardson, "Bylaws for Public Library Boards," Library of Michigan, May 1999. http://www.michigan.gov/hal/0,1607,7-160-17451_18668_18689-54440—,00.html. Accessed April 4, 2007.

2. Glendale Public Library Board, www.glendaleaz.com/boardsandcommissions/LibraryAdvisoryBoard.cfm. Accessed April 4, 2007.

3. Minneapolis Public Library Board of Trustees, www.ci.minneapolis.mn.us/boards-and-commissions/Library-Bd-of-Trustees.asp. Accessed April 4, 2007.

4. Plant City Public Library Board, www.plantcitygov.com/boards/plctybl1.htm. Accessed February 28, 2007.

5. Pocahontas Public Library Board, www.pocahontas.lib.ia.us/library-information/library-board. Accessed February 28, 2007.

6. Monona Public Library Board, http://www.monona.wi.us/index.asp?Type=B_BASIC&SEC={C270FF62-029D-441B-BFF0-A3A7BB125958}. Accessed February 28, 2007.

7. Enid Public Library Board, www.enid.org/boards/library.htm. Accessed February 28, 2007.

8. Library of Virginia, http://www.lva.lib.va.us/whoweare/boards/liboard. htm. Accessed February 28, 2007.

9. Longmont Public Library Board, http://204.133.207.2/boards/directory/ library.htm. Accessed February 28, 2007.

10. Ferndale Public Library Board, www.ferndale-mi.com/Government/ BoardsandCommissions.htm#Library. Accessed February 28, 2007.

11. Santa Barbara Public Library Board, www.santabarbaraca.gov/Gov ernment/Boards_and_Commissions_D-M/Library_Board/. Accessed February 28, 2007.

12. Franklin Public Library Board, www.franklin.ma.us/town/library/ libboards.htm. Accessed February 28, 2007.

13. Scottsdale Public Library Board, http://www.scottsdaleaz.gov/boards/ library.asp. Accessed July 19, 2007.

CHAPTER 8

Your Customers: Your Reason to Exist

Be everywhere, do everything, and never fail to astonish
the customer.
—Margaret Metchell, first American female retail executive.
[It became the motto for Macy's Department Stores.]

Above all else, remember that your customers are the reason you exist. (*Customers, patrons, users:* Usage of the terms varies from region to region and even library to library, and we use them interchangeably.) The library is there because *they* want a library. The library is a service organization, and its sole purpose is to serve. Historically, public libraries came into existence as a way for members of the community to share resources so that each community member wouldn't have to purchase the same books. By sharing their books, budget dollars could stretch farther and each community member could have access to a greater number of resources.

As libraries grew over the years, the idea of having a professional staff came into existence. People began to realize that certain services could be better offered by a trained professional; thus, the concept of a professional librarian was born. From the beginning, the idea has been that this trained librarian is a public servant, a lesson we must never forget.

Even if you don't see yourself as a public servant, your library users do. Therefore, it's best for you to assume the role proactively and meet—or better yet, exceed—user expectations.

WHO ARE YOUR CUSTOMERS?

Who are your customers? Historically, it was easy to define a customer as anyone who walks in the door. Later, that concept was extended to include those seeking external service, such as telephone reference or interlibrary loan. Today, many patrons use the library and its resources without ever setting foot inside the building. People around the world can be our customers.

But let's focus on our primary users, those who live and work in our community. Though some may choose to define these as persons who hold library cards, it seems logical that we should extend that a bit and say that our primary customers are our taxpayers—those who pay for the library with their tax dollars—and their families.

Our local customers, then, are represented by some sort of governing body to whom we are responsible, most likely in the guise of a library board, mayor and council, or the like. It is vital to our existence, then, that we listen to these people, both directly and through their duly elected or appointed representatives.

HOW WILL YOU GET FEEDBACK FROM YOUR CUSTOMERS?

If we are to listen to our patrons, how do we hear from them? The short answer is any time and any way we can. However, there is much to gain by taking a proactive approach and actively gathering input from those we are appointed to serve.

SUGGESTION BOX

One way to gather input from patrons that has been used successfully is a suggestion box. Simply place a suggestion box somewhere in the library where patrons can have access to it. We offer the following suggestions for the box:

- Keep the suggestion box someplace where it will be easily accessible to users but where those who wish to remain anonymous can quietly use it without drawing attention to themselves. We must note that there is an inherent risk in allowing anonymous suggestions: You may hear things you don't wish to hear. Some may be personally offensive or even abusive. In other words, hiding behind the cloak of anonymity, someone may say abusive things about you or about your staff. However, we feel that the advantages far outweigh the drawbacks. We suggest you just toughen up and be ready to accept what you get; consider that some of the more unkind things may be written in anger, and deal with them as such. If unkind things are written about staff members that otherwise have no substantiation, destroy them. It's better to destroy a note written in anger than to destroy the morale of a trustworthy staff member. Some librarians find that they are able to keep things on a more positive note by placing a sign near the box that reads, "We will respond personally to suggestions if you give us your contact information," or something similar.
- Make your suggestion box lockable. Suggestions should not be available to anyone who chooses to dip a hand in it. They should be reserved for your eyes or those of your designee. In some cases, the library board chooses to gather and read the suggestions first, passing on to you, the director, those they deem appropriate.
- Keep a pencil and suggestion forms by the box.
- Check it on a regular basis.
- If you're not prepared to deal appropriately with the suggestions you get, don't have a box.

CONVERSATIONS

Talk to your patrons. Don't be nosy, but show that you value them as people. If they mention their family, try to remember the details and ask about their family the next time you see them. If they mention hobbies or specific interests, introduce those topics into future conversations.

Reference staff and, often, circulation staff are in a position to get to know the patrons and their interests. If they determine, for example, that Mary Smith is an avid gardener, they (or you) can use that knowledge to ask Ms. Smith what she thinks of your collection of gardening books and ask her if there are items she thinks might be added to the collection. Likewise, staff can use that information to suggest items in the collection that she may have overlooked but which would be of interest to her. This approach also works well in the fiction section, where your staff might be weak in an area, such as western novels.

Try to get to know library patrons in other settings. You may be able to gather more useful information in a more social setting. If the library has social gatherings, such as a film showing or a reception for a new board member, use the occasion to mingle. Be inquisitive. Ask people leading, open-ended questions. Engage them in conversation. Then, use what you have learned to improve library service.

SURVEYS

A more formalized method for gathering information is the user survey. In order to gather useful information, a survey must be well designed. If you are inexperienced in designing surveys, it may be desirable at this point to hire an outside consultant. If you decide to design your own survey, consider the following:

1. What is the purpose of this survey?
2. What information do you hope to gather?
3. How will you analyze the results? Who will have that responsibility? Is that person qualified to do so?
4. How will you use the information you learn? What difference will it make in the library? If the survey results won't produce a difference in the library, don't do the survey!
5. Which user group do you need to target: all users or just some of them? How large a sample do you need to obtain a reliable result?
6. What is your methodology for conducting the survey? For example, will you ask people at the door? Will you mail the surveys? Will you leaving them lying around so only interested people pick them up?
7. Keep the survey brief so that it is not burdensome for the respondents. It is probably better to do several surveys spread out over time than one long survey that will be difficult or time-consuming for respondents.

8. Test the survey instrument ahead of time. Try to have a small group respond to the survey to determine if you are getting the type of responses you need. Are respondents able to understand the questions? Do they interpret them as you had hoped they would?

9. Determine when you need to ask open-ended questions and when to ask simple yes/no or ranking questions. A question such as "On a scale of 1 to 10, how happy are you with library services" may tell you that users are happy or unhappy, but it does nothing to tell you why or why not unless you ask follow-up questions.

FOCUS GROUPS

Another very useful technique for gathering information from your patrons is through focus groups. A focus group is a technique for gathering information by inviting a small group of people, representative of a larger group, to dialogue with you. A moderator asks questions while a recorder notes the answers. Here are some tips:

1. Determine which group you need input from: all your users, or a subset, such as mothers of toddlers?

2. Determine how you will select a representative sample of that group.

3. Reward the participants for coming, perhaps in the form of food.

4. Have two people host the meeting: a facilitator and a recorder.

5. Encourage people to be candid. Assure them that no names will be associated with the comments. What happens in this room stays in this room.

6. Use an outside facilitator and recorder if at all possible so people will feel free to be more candid. People might find it hard to criticize the library in front of someone who works there.

STAYING IN TOUCH BY WORKING THE PUBLIC DESKS

Let's face it: We get so caught up in our administrative duties that we sometimes get out of touch with our users. An excellent remedy for that is to work the public desks. Whether you do so regularly or sporadically, of course, depends on the workflow in your library, but we encourage you to do so on a fairly frequent basis.

- *Reference desk.* By working the reference desk, you will get to know patrons and their needs for information. It's a great opportunity to demonstrate that you, like your staff, are there to help them. Having patrons come to you for help is a great conversation starter and can give you topics to speak to the patron about in other situations in the future, as well as giving you useful information about what patrons need.

- *Circulation.* Conversation at the circulation desk is much less focused than at the reference desk. It may range from comments about the weather to some happening in the community. It's a great way to meet patrons in an interchange that's probably much less intense than a reference interview. Working the circulation desk can also become a sort of readers' advisory. Patrons may ask you what you've been reading lately or what book you'd recommend to them, so be prepared! Also, working the circulation desk will give you a firsthand look at what items and types of items are in demand at the library (not to mention that it demonstrates to your staff that you're willing to pitch in and lend a hand just like they are expected to do).

- *Youth and children.* Even the young patrons have opinions about library materials and services. And you're more likely to get a forthright response!

PAYING ATTENTION TO STATISTICS

What type of statistics do or should you keep? That's one of the first things you need to learn as a new director. Who gathers those statistics? How, when, where are they gathered? Where are they kept? How are they compiled and how often? What use is made of them?

Once you've answered those questions, you need to determine what data you need that's not being collected. Why isn't it? Is it feasible to do so? How would you go about collecting it?

The next step is to determine what data is being collected that you don't need to collect. Unless your library is overstaffed, there may be better uses of your time.

Likewise, determine if potentially useful data is being collected but not being used. If it's not being used, why not? What must you do to turn this raw data into useful information?

We must confess that we're big on statistics. While statistics often don't give the complete picture, they can be used to support other types of information. They're also useful at budget time.

For example, circulation statistics can tell you what's circulating and what's not. You may suspect that travel books circulate more in the summer; statistics can confirm it (or not). While it is likely that tree identification or "leaf" books circulate more in October in certain parts of the country, statistics can confirm it. A longitudinal look at the October statistics will show you that this is an annual occurrence. Then you can use this information for acquisitions in August to make sure you will have enough "leaf books" to meet the demand before October rolls around.

Likewise, statistics may tell you that your audiocassettes no longer circulate, or that they are still very popular. In turn, that information can be used to make weeding decisions.

If statistics show that your books on tape have experienced a huge drop in circulation but that all three of your audiobooks in MP3 format are constantly out, it may be time to increase your holdings in that area. Having such information shows you how to allocate your budget for the greatest patron satisfaction.

Gathering attendance figures can show you when the library is busy and when things are slow. While an automatic gate counter can give you total attendance figures, an hourly attendance count can show you *when* the library is busy. We suggest an actual walk-around head count each hour. Having such information can often provide support in making service decisions. For example, if you receive a request to extend hours, such as keeping the library open until 10:00 P.M., a look at the hourly attendance figures will show that such action may not be justified because the library is sparsely used after 8:00 P.M.

IN SUMMARY

The purpose of the library is to provide excellent library service to your community. As clichéd as it sounds, the customer should always come first. You need to see which services and resources are being used and which aren't, so you can allocate funds in a responsible manner. Communicate with your customers directly one-on-one and in focus groups as well as through suggestion boxes and surveys to get their input. Statistics are useful when tracking usage. They are also vital during budget hearings.

CHAPTER 9

Key People in the Community:
No Library Is an Island

Never forget that you're a member of your own community.
Don't do something that you wouldn't like to see done.
—Keith Richman, Californian politician

The library is not an entity unto itself but a very important member of the community, and a cooperative relationship is essential. One of the first things you need to do as a new director is discern the library's role in that community and determine what your personal role as a community member will be. Start by getting to know the key players.

What people and organizations are leaders in your community? To learn who the key players are, it may be helpful to define the roles they play. Let's take a look at some of them.

POLITICAL LEADERS

While the degree to which local politics affect the library may vary from community to community, there is, by definition, some effect. Who is closest to the library? The mayor? The city manager? The council members? Figure out not only who controls the budget for the library but who within your community may have an influential role on it. For example, it may be the city council, not the mayor, that sets the library budget. But the mayor may have enormous influence with the council on setting the budget and may even have the final vote. Things of this nature may not be "official," and you probably won't find a record of them anywhere, but your knowing them can prove tremendously important for the library. Understand where the power is, and use this knowledge to keep your library in good standing. If the mere thought of politics makes you ill, you should reconsider being a library director; it is a very political job, even in small libraries.

Likewise, the library may have an "enemy" or, at least, someone who's not friendly toward it out there somewhere in a very influential position. Find out who that person is, what the issues with the library are, and work with that person in overcoming the obstacle. Sometimes, that obstacle is as obvious as a council member who feels that on the funding totem pole, the library should be at the very bottom, because after all, in this person's opinion, it's "just a bunch of books." You'll need to demonstrate to this person the other roles of the library, including its position as the community's major source of information, the place for online access, and the focal point of community meetings and educational programming.

LOCAL MEDIA

What are the local media in your town? Is there a newspaper? Is it a daily or weekly? Who owns it? Who is the editor-in-chief? Who's the reporter assigned to local government? Historically, what has been their relationship with the library?

Does your community have a TV station? A radio station? A local magazine? What has been their attitude toward the library?

Has the library been using the local media? How? If the library hasn't been working with the local media up to now, you need to start. The media are always looking for good local stories, and nobody has more stories than the library. (Sorry.) But the local media are usually willing, often even eager, to publish stories about the library if you will provide them.

If no local newspaper or TV or radio station exist, consider how to put information into the more regional newspaper that your local citizens read. Some regionals may have a page for your local town, but even if they don't, they are often glad to receive news from the towns they serve.

If you have them, visit the local newspaper and TV or radio station. Inquire if there's a contact person charged with writing about local government or the library specifically. Ask, "Whose beat is the library on?" Then, make contact with that person. Ask what kind of news from the library is of interest. Ask if you can submit library news without waiting to be asked. Ask if there's a predetermined format. Is there a deadline by when news needs to be submitted?

Perhaps there is someone on the library staff (or board) who is especially talented at putting together press releases and news items. Make sure that this person is introduced to the appropriate contact person from each media outlet in the community. It's also important for you as director to sign off on the press releases so you won't be blindsided. For example, it's really easy for the media to take a press release about the library getting a new security system and spin it into "Local library loses hundreds of books a year."

SCHOOL LIBRARIANS, TEACHERS, AND PRINCIPALS IN THE LOCAL SCHOOLS

It is vital that the library have good relations with the schools in the community. After all, their students make up a large portion of your users. Many a public library has been blindsided by teachers giving an assignment to a great number of students, whose needs have quickly overwhelmed the library's resources. An open, cooperative relationship with the local schools, school librarians, and as many individual teachers as possible can help preclude such situations. If teachers are familiar with your library, its staff, and its resources, they are more likely to work cooperatively. Just as it is easier for you to call someone you know than someone you don't, so it is for teachers; they are more likely to call someone they know at the library to ask for help or to give a heads-up on an assignment than they are to call someone who's just an anonymous voice on the phone.

The key message for you to give to the schools is "What we can do for you?" Ask the school librarian to help you let teachers and principals know what the library can do for them. Advertise the library's services to them any way you can. Tell them not only what the library can do, but what the library's expectations are to make a cooperative relationship work better for all. For example, if teachers are going to make an assignment that will require library resources, how would you like them to communicate that to the library? Through their school librarian? A phone call? An e-mail? To whom should they direct it? Provide them with a list of contacts and a set of guidelines. Make it as easy for them as you possibly can, and in doing so, you'll make it easier on your staff.

Visits to the schools in your community, public and private, are an effective way to advertise your summer reading program. The easiest way to do this is to have the school librarian invite you into the school. You may need to gain permission to enter the schools. When permission is granted, the librarian, principal, or individual teachers will gather the children together for you, and you provide a whopping good storytime and hand out summer reading club flyers. We still remember as clear as day, many years later, the "library lady" who came to our elementary school each month to read a story to our class; she may have had a great influence on our choosing this profession.

HEAD START

Why is a good relationship with the Head Start program important for the library? Because these children are the readers and library users of tomorrow and the library supporters of next week.

But you also need to ask why the library is important to Head Start. If you believe that part of the mission of the library is to teach and encourage people to read, it should be obvious. If it is part of the library's mission to create lifelong learners, it is never too young to start. Many of the children in Head Start come from disadvantaged backgrounds; a good relationship between the two organizations can go a long way in helping children overcome those obstacles.

Work with the administrators and teachers at Head Start to see if there are specific ways you can serve these children. Can the library conduct a storytime at the Head Start center each week or each month? Or can the kids visit the library on a field trip? Can you send over a rotating collection of books for use at the center? Can you conduct any training sessions for Head Start teachers in getting children ready for school?

BOY SCOUTS AND GIRL SCOUTS

Boy and Girl Scouts, when properly supervised, can be an excellent source of energetic assistance. Even Cub Scouts and Brownies can be trained to clean books, and they often find it great fun to do so. In one library, a Scout raised money to buy a complete set of merit badge books for the collection.

SENIOR CENTERS

Your local senior center can serve as a channel through which you can offer many services to senior citizens. For example, you might help form a book club there. You might deliver a box or two of books on a regular basis for seniors to read. Or, you might sponsor book review sessions. Also, through the senior center, you might learn about those who would benefit from your homebound services.

Senior centers are great places to advertise for volunteers. We've been very pleased with our older volunteers. In fact, we've even had a few retired librarians help us!

LITERACY VOLUNTEERS

Is there a group of literacy volunteers within your community? Is it a formal or informal group? Perhaps they have been using the library for years, but if not, how can you contact them?

What roles can the library play in working with literacy volunteers? For many libraries the primary role is providing a place for literacy instructors and students to meet. Obviously, the secondary role is providing reading materials. Sometimes these adult literacy students are embarrassed by their lack of reading and writing skills; by providing a safe atmosphere in which to learn, libraries can provide the encouragement they need.

Some libraries encourage their staff to volunteer as literacy instructors and will allow a defined number of hours per week of staff time for such an activity.

NEARBY BUSINESS OWNERS

What types of businesses are near the library? What needs do they have? How can you determine how the library can help meet those needs? They best way to find out is by talking to the business owners and employees.

Is there a history of problems between the library and local businesses that you need to know about? For example, are local business customers and library patrons always fighting for limited parking spaces? How can you work together to solve the problem and make things better for everyone?

Having a good relationship with local businesses can often come back as a positive benefit to the library. These businesses are willing to support the library in many ways, such as providing prizes for summer reading programs. In some libraries, businesses have purchased plastic covers for the current issues of magazines (which protects them and helps keep them from walking out the door). The benefit to the business is free advertising in exchange for the free covers; their logo appears on the cover.

NEARBY CHURCHES, SYNAGOGUES, AND MOSQUES

Why would the library need to befriend churches, synagogues, and mosques? One good reason is resource sharing. Public libraries tend not to have in-depth collections in the area of religion, while these other groups are likely to have very in-depth collections in those areas. By fomenting good relations with these organizations, libraries may have access to resources for their patrons that they would not otherwise have. Some churches, synagogues, and mosques may be willing to lend directly to members of the general public; otherwise, their items may be available through interlibrary loan.

If there is a librarian at the congregation, this person may be an invaluable resource at the time your library is building its collection in the area of religion. Perhaps there is no one on the staff of your library with expertise in the area of religion generally or in a specific religion. Nearby congregational librarians can provide much advice. But why would they? What is the "Scratch my back, I'll scratch yours" payoff for them? Congregational libraries often have notoriously small, even nonexistent, acquisitions budgets. If the public library can purchase some of the resources these librarians recommend, members of the congregation can have their needs met that way. And what is the payoff for the public library in return for spending their budget on resources of this type? New and satisfied patrons! Remember that the members of that local congregation are also your supporters, the taxpayers!

Sometimes patrons come to the public library on a spiritual or emotional quest. It is the role of the public library to provide resources, but not spiritual guidance. By having good relations with nearby congregations, a referral can be made to the local congregation when appropriate.

LOCAL COLLEGES

College students often look to the public library to meet their need for academic resources. While the two types of libraries focus on different "markets" and collect different types of resources, students and members of the general public often do not know that and expect the public library to be able to meet their needs. In cases where the public library cannot do so, it is helpful if the public librarians, particularly the reference librarians, are familiar with the nearby academic collections so that students and faculty can be referred there.

Similarly, students from a college or university that is *not* nearby may be home for the weekend or summer vacation in your town. They expect your library to meet their needs because they are not near their academic library, which may be hundreds, or thousands, of miles away. Having a good relationship with a nearby academic institution will allow you to borrow resources through interlibrary loan (time permitting, and if you offer that service for out-of-town students) that are not in your collection. Likewise, knowing the collections of nearby institutions and their policies will help you know when to refer people there.

Having a good working relationship with nearby academic librarians will give you some insight into how your library can meet the needs of their students and the knowledge of when to refer your patrons to them. Likewise, through an open relationship, the academic librarians will have a better idea of which types of resources your library is able to provide and which not.

SCHOOL LIBRARIES

A good relationship with nearby school librarians enables you to better serve their libraries' patrons and, in turn, allows them to better serve your young patrons. After all, these patrons are one and the same! Additionally, it is their taxes and those paid by their parents that support both libraries. Both libraries have a commitment to serve these young users.

Having a good working relationship with local school librarians will allow you both to do a better job. The school librarians, as stated earlier, may be able to give you a heads-up when teachers are making specific assignments, thus allowing you to have resources prepared when the flood of students hits your library. In many parts of the country, for example, science teachers give their students assignments in leaf identification each fall. At other times, teachers may assign students to prepare a project for the science fair or some other type of fair. By knowing in advance when students will be wanting these types of resources, you may seek them out, gather them together, and place them on limited reserve—whatever will serve your young users best.

Similarly, by having an open relationship with the school librarians, you can let them know which types of resources and services you are or are not able to provide. If, for example, you do not have a collection supporting science fair projects, you can let the school librarians know that, and they can relay to their teachers to tell students not to depend on the public library for this type of information.

By working with school librarians, you can share collection development. You may collect a few titles in science fair projects, and they may collect a few; but by working together, you can avoid duplication and provide twice as many titles for your users.

If you notice that students from a particular class are coming to your library and they do not have adequate research skills, you can relay that information to the school librarian, who may then provide the needed instruction or work with the classroom teacher to teach these skills.

Public libraries and school libraries often have diverging philosophies of services. It is usually the philosophy of the public library to just give the user the information, while it is the philosophy of the school library to teach students information skills so they can find it for themselves; they don't just give them the answer. Working in conjunction, you can provide the service that teachers want for their students and thus not short-circuit the lesson of learning the research skills rather than just getting an answer.

Don't overlook interlibrary loan. Can your library develop an intergovernmental interlibrary loan agreement, sometimes called an interlocal agreement, with the school district? What will you lend to the schools? What can they lend you? While interlibrary loan is fairly commonplace in public libraries, it's important for you to understand that schools are sometimes afraid of interlibrary loan because they fear it will deplete their already meager collections. Work with the school librarians to make sure they understand that they can always say no to a particular request with no hard feelings. For example, many schools refuse interlibrary requests for tree-identification, or "leaf books," or Halloween books in October because those materials are in heavy demand by their own students.

A few years ago in Indianapolis, a prototype information-sharing project named *Project Hi-Net* was developed among the schools and the public library. The countywide public library offered to host the online catalog for all 31 high schools—public, private, parochial, and institutional—in the county. So that the general public would not deplete the small collections of the high schools, it was agreed that members of the public could not borrow from the schools except under limited circumstances, but students could borrow freely from the public library. To facilitate access to resources in this large county where many students had limited transportation, it was agreed that resources from other schools and the public library would be delivered to the requesting school. Because the public library had trucks and vans crisscrossing the county each day to service its branches, daily delivery service to the high schools was established via a formal agreement for service, and grant funding was obtained to pay the costs of the service. The resulting benefit to students was incalculable. While your library may be more remote or have fewer resources, a similar project is possible!

OTHER PUBLIC LIBRARIES

If you are fortunate enough to be in an area where there are other public libraries, it is imperative to have good working relationships among you. If you serve similar types of communities, you can increase the availability of resources to your patrons by providing a greater quantity of resources than any of you could alone. If you serve diverse communities, you can enrich the lives of your patrons by providing more resources of different types than any of you would alone.

It is important to develop agreements among yourselves as to how you will cooperate. These agreements may be formal or informal. They include such issues as interlibrary loan, reciprocal borrowing, and service to patrons.

Service to Patrons of Other Libraries

Your library needs to have a policy outlining the services it will give to patrons of other libraries. For example, will your library offer interlibrary loan service to those who don't hold one of *your* library cards? What about the aforementioned students home for the holidays? Will you provide reference service to patrons from other libraries, and to what extent?

All these issues need to be negotiated mutually with other libraries through intergovernmental agreement so that service is equitable. If libraries are providing different levels of service (i.e., much service at one library but very little at another), there will likely be problems in the future.

Interlibrary Loan

Interlibrary loan, as the name implies, means that one library lends items to another. Even though the item in question is for the use of a patron, the agreement itself is between libraries. If your library borrows an item from Library A, lends it to your patron, and your patron loses it, it is *your* obligation to pay for or replace that item for Library A. You may then decide whether or not to charge the patron for the lost or damaged item. For this reason, it is desirable to have a written interlibrary loan policy for patrons, noting their obligation to your library and your library's obligation to the lending library. The latter may be part of your intergovernmental agreement.

You interlibrary loan agreement should detail which types of items you will request (from another library) for your patrons and/ or which types of items you will *not* request. It should also describe which types of items you will or will not lend to another library. Interlibrary loan policy has some obvious exceptions, such as antiquarian books, reference books, and current bestsellers, but they need to be specified in the agreement. You would not want to tell your local users you've sent all the bestsellers to another library. Many libraries are reluctant to share nonprint media, such as DVDs, tapes, and CDs, through interlibrary loan.

After all the legal agreements have been signed and interlibrary loan goes into effect, you'll see how beneficial it is. If you're a small library with a low book budget, you'll be able to get materials for your customers you couldn't otherwise afford. You can also make a contribution to the interlibrary system, even if you have a limited collection. You might have resources that are of particular interest to other libraries, such as a well-developed collection of western novels, inspirational fiction, or Latino poetry.

Your policy also needs to state that you can say no to any request at any time for any reason. You may not want to lend a particular book, for example, because after years of oblivion, it has suddenly become popular with your patrons. This often happens if an author appears on television or makes a local appearance or if a book has been made into a movie. And you often will receive interlibrary loan requests for materials of this type because the same items have become popular at other libraries for the same reasons, exhausting their collections. Once again, do you really want to tell your customers you've sent all these "hot" titles to another library? Of course, you won't want to say no to a loan any more often than necessary or your library will get the reputation of being uncooperative and other libraries won't want to lend to you. Your policy needs to state the cost of replacing a lost or damaged item. The cost may be based on what the resource originally cost, its replacement cost in today's market, or, sometimes, a flat figure, such as $50 per book. Many libraries include some type of processing fee on top of the cost of the item to cover the expense of getting the item shelf ready: plastic cover, cataloging costs, barcodes, spine labels, and so forth. Replaced books don't just automatically fly to the shelf; there is often a heavy cost involved in preparing items for circulation.

Your policy should state the circulation period for specific types of items and any fines involved for overdues. For example, your policy may be to lend a book for three weeks but a magazine issue for only a week or not at all. Borrowing libraries need to know this.

Your policy needs to specifically address articles from journals and magazines. Do you lend whole issues? Do you photocopy articles and send the photocopy? Do you mail or fax them? Or, are you in a position to scan articles and send them via e-mail? The policy must also address copyright concerns. What about articles from databases? You need to know what your EULA (End-User License Agreement) allows you to do.

In writing an interlibrary loan policy, you must always keep in mind the matter of copyright. Copyright is not an easy issue to address. It's murky and constantly changing. It's like trying to nail Jell-O to the wall. But as director, it is your responsibility to stay on top of copyright issues and make sure the library functions within the law and guidelines. Make sure that those directly responsible for interlibrary loan, both coming and going, are on top of current copyright legislation.

Additionally, your interlibrary loan policy needs to address what will happen if your patron borrows an item you have gotten from another library and keeps it past its due date. Do you issue an overdue notice? Recall the item? Charge a huge fine? Determine at what point and under what circumstances an overdue item is considered a lost item and gets billed to the patron.

Since an interlibrary loan agreement is an intergovernmental agreement, it will probably need to be approved by your mayor, council, city or town manager, or other government official. Whatever you do, don't present it for approval before your chain of command, as well as your organization's attorney, have seen it and given it the green light!

Statewide Networks

Every state has either a statewide or a regional library network, maybe both. Learn which networks are available in your area and how you can become an active participant.

Pennsylvania, for example, has a statewide program, Access Pennsylvania, which includes a statewide library card and the Power Library, an online resource. Funded by the legislature and LSTA funding, citizens of Pennsylvania are allowed to borrow materials from any library and return them to their own library. These are returned to the original library free of charge for all parties. Such funding allows the legislature to provide a service to every citizen in the state at a very cost-effective use of tax dollars.

Reciprocal Borrowing

Reciprocal borrowing essentially means allowing patrons from another library to walk into your library and borrow an item. You may issue them one of your library cards after proper identification, or you may allow them to borrow based on the card from their home library. Or, you may not allow reciprocal borrowing at all. This needs to be negotiated as part of any intergovernmental agreements you may have. Reciprocity, of course, means that your patrons can borrow from the other library under the same terms that their patrons can borrow from yours.

You must also determine if a fee is to be charged for the privilege of reciprocal borrowing and, if so, how much. In some cases a patron may be considered out of district and the fee for borrowing may be quite steep—equivalent to the amount of property tax paid by residents for library service.

Sometimes reciprocal borrowing is negotiated at a higher level than an interlocal agreement. Some states have a statewide borrower's card, allowing a patron from any public library to borrow resources from any other public library in the state. Sometimes a fee is charged for the card.

OTHER CITY/TOWN/COUNTY DEPARTMENTS

Within your community, as in every community, there are a number of other government offices with which you need to develop a relationship. Remember that the library is a service organization; not providing excellent services to other organizations that form part of your government can have many negative repercussions, particularly financial ones, for the library. On the other hand, a positive relationship can be mutually beneficial. Let's look at some of these departments and how you might work with them.

Human Resources

Whether you're hiring, firing, reclassifying, or training employees, the human resources department is a vital partner in your decision-making processes. They can make sure that what you've done or, better yet, what you're about to do is legal and fair.

Social Services

An important government department to work with is social services. Some members of your community may be clients of social services because they're in need of a job. The library can provide many of the resources that these community members need for a successful job search. Let social services know what your resources are and that you're willing to help. Perhaps you might even want to create a flyer that you can place at the social services office listing job resources that are available at the library. Remember that an employed citizen is a taxpayer—and taxes support the library. Similarly, if patrons come into the library for a job search, you may be able to refer them to social services for assistance.

Some libraries, particularly those in urban areas, have a large homeless population. For many reasons, social services can provide much-valued assistance for the library in dealing with these individuals.

CULTURAL ORGANIZATIONS

Cultural organizations, such as the Polish American Club, can be of great assistance when you're developing a foreign-language collection or putting together a program on diverse cultures. We have, on occasion, called these cultural organizations when we've had a patron who couldn't communicate in English, and they've acted as interpreters.

SERVICE ORGANIZATIONS

In every community there are numerous service organizations. Many of these organizations have regular meetings for which they are sometimes looking for speakers or presenters. Get to know them; let them know who at the library can speak and what topics they can speak about. Is the library offering a new service? Have you recently implemented a new technology (such as a new database of interest to the business community)? Many members of the service organizations would love to hear about these services. These meetings are great forums for publicizing the library's services!

Many service organizations sponsor projects that can be useful to the library or in which the library may support the organization. In fact, service organizations are often looking for beneficial projects to fund. Call each organization in turn and ask how you can work with them. If you're asking for funds, have a specific project in mind, not just "money for the library."

In Glendale, Arizona, the Fraternal Order of Eagles gave money every year to help fund the large-print collection at their local branch.

Another example of a service organization that works with libraries is the Lions Club, which collects used eyeglasses for distribution to those in need. Some libraries have placed collection barrels inside the library where visitors can deposit their old glasses. We bet that when the library needs some strong backs to help spruce up the exterior of the building, they don't have to ask twice to get some volunteers from the local Lions Club!

Rotary, Soroptomists, Altrusa, American Association of University Women (AAUW), Kiwanis, and Elks are only a few of the other organizations with which you can partner. When one of these groups helps your library, be sure to thank them with a letter and mention them in any press releases you write about the gift or service.

RETIRED SENIOR VOLUNTEER PROGRAM (RSVP)

Another organization with which the library can have a mutually beneficial relationship is the Retired Senior Volunteer Program. For more information on the RSVP, see chapter 6.

SMALL BUSINESS ASSOCIATION (SBA)

Many communities have a Small Business Association (SBA). The library *is* a small business. The local SBA may be able to offer assistance with the business end of the library, such as the marketing of services, or the financial end. They may be able to provide a volunteer to help with the library's financial records, and although we don't normally recommend using a volunteer for bookkeeping tasks, some very small libraries may have few options.

CHAMBER OF COMMERCE

You need to have a good working relationship with the chamber of commerce. Some libraries are official members of their local chamber.

In many areas, particularly those that attract a number of tourists, the Chamber, or its tourism division, provides information on the local community. If they produce a packet of information, why not include the library? The library may display this information on a rack readily available to patrons and visitors. This information, including the information about the library, may reach not only tourists who visit the area only once or a few times, but it may be given to those who are planning to move into the community and will become future library patrons. Before deciding to move into a community, people often want to know about its churches, schools, and libraries!

Remember also that you will be hiring as positions in the library become vacant, and perhaps interviewing candidates who are not familiar with your area. As part of the hiring process, you need to convince your choice candidates that your town is a desirable place for them and their families. We have had good experiences working with the local chamber to get promotional packets to give to our prospective employees. These packets contain information on items of varied interest, such as local attractions, schools, churches, real estate, and, of course, the library!

HOSPITALS AND CLINICS

While libraries often have patrons in need of medical information, a public library can't be expected to collect extensively in that area. Libraries in nearby hospitals and clinics, on the other hand, collect broadly and deeply in the area of health sciences. Having a good relationship with these institutions will allow you to refer patrons to those libraries or to borrow items from them via interlibrary loan.

IN SUMMARY

Communities have many diverse organizations. Each one fills a particular niche. By developing good relationships with them, a library can increase its area of service and, in turn, increase its access to resources of many types. These organizations and their members are your taxpayers and supporters. Having positive relationships with them, as well as with other libraries and other departments in your organization, is vital to the health of your library.

CHAPTER 10

Managing Change: Look Before You Leap!

> The main dangers in this life are the people who want to change everything—or nothing.
>
> —Nancy Astor (1879–1964)

Change will happen. Change *must* happen. Prepare for it. Plan for it!

Change can be both exciting and discomfiting. Some people thrive on it, and some people resist it. You are likely to be surrounded by people of both types. Part of your responsibility as director is to determine who falls into which camp and to work *with* them. You must also determine which type of person *you* are and keep your natural tendencies in balance.

The first step is to make sure that you have a solid base: a context within which to manage change. Understand the local community as well as the library and the profession within which it operates. You also need to know the major issues of the day affecting the profession: For example, be aware of the graying of the profession and how it will impact the future of your library. Be aware of newly emerging technologies and how they might be applied in the library, *your* library.

In order to stay current, stay professionally active and in touch, a topic covered elsewhere in this book.

Why were you hired? Were you hired to make changes? What kind of changes? New directors may sometimes find themselves between the proverbial rock and a hard place: Those to whom you report may *want* you to make changes; the staff, on the other hand, with whom you must work day to day, may be happy with the status quo and resistant to change. On the other hand, it is not an unknown situation for the library staff to be expecting the new director to bring about immediate change, while the board may like the way things have always been done.

Getting caught in the middle is a surefire recipe for disaster. As director, you are responsible to the people who hired you, whether it's a library board, a town or city manager, a county supervisor—whoever. They hired you, and they can dismiss you. On the other hand, upsetting the staff with change, or the lack thereof, can create enemies within, generate complaints to the board, and eventually cost you your job. It is extremely important that you, as the new director, avoid getting caught in a struggle between feuding factions: those who want immediate, sweeping changes and those who want none.

It is vital that you understand the reasons to change or not change. The first question to ask is why. Then listen carefully to the responses. Is change necessary? Change for change's sake is generally not a good thing. You need to understand which changes should be made in order to "sell" the changes to those who are resistant.

If you were hired as a change agent, whoever hired you expects to see some changes almost immediately. Staff, on the other hand, may be resistant. Some of them may regard you as an outsider who wants to come in and change *their* library. From the very beginning, you must begin to preach the message that this is *our* library, that you are all on the same team, and that your goal is what's best for the library.

HOW TO START MAKING CHANGE

The best way to start making changes is by gathering information. Make sure you have enough information before making a decision. Is the change necessary? Why or why not? Who will be affected by this change? How will they be affected? How widespread should the change be? Can or should it be partially implemented or implemented in phases? Is there a best time to implement the change? Who is in favor of the change? Why? Who opposes it? Why?

While you are gathering information, make sure you listen to everyone who has something to say. Hear them out and show respect for their point of view. Be open to compromise. Be willing to change your own ideas if their suggestions are in the best interest of the library. If others are directly affected by the change, make sure you involve them in the decision-making process. If you give everyone a fair listen, you will earn their respect and gain much ground, even if the final decision you make doesn't agree with their point of view.

Can the decision be made by a group, rather than by you alone? Is that a better way to make the decision? Can the decision be made by consensus? These are all questions you need to ask yourself.

Once a decision has been made or, even better, before it has been finalized, make sure everyone understands the rationale upon which the decision was based. A clear understanding of the "whys" by everyone can often defuse a difficult situation. Such an understanding makes it easier for others to accept the decision, especially when it does not agree with their suggestions.

Any decision must be well founded on the basics. Is it supportive of the library's mission statement? If the library has a formalized vision statement, will this decision work toward achieving that vision? Does the library have a long-range plan? Does this decision fit within that plan? Which of the library's goals and objectives will this decision help you reach? How?

BENCHMARKING YOUR PROGRESS

Benchmarking is one way to assess your processes at the library. It's a method of comparing what you do against what those who are considered the "best of the best" do. Some organizations use a 5-point approach, while others use a 7-point method. The Xerox Corporation originated a 10-point approach. It doesn't matter which process you use, as long as you hit all the key elements. We have used both the 7-point and the 10-point method, and although they both work well, the 7-point method is slightly easier to follow.

Point 1. Decide what task you want to benchmark.
Point 2. Analyze the way your library performs this task. Break it down into small steps. Flowcharts can help.
Point 3. Call your colleagues, do database searches, look through journals, call your state library, and contact state and national library associations to find out who's considered the

best in the field in performing this particular task. These will be your benchmarking partners, or the organizations you'll measure yourself against.

Point 4. Find out how your benchmarking partners perform the task you're evaluating. This will involve phone calls, e-mails, site visits, and so on. Site visits are the best. If you can, observe the process firsthand.

Point 5. Compare their processes to yours. Be critical, and don't make excuses for yourself while you do this comparison. You may discover that your process is better than those you've observed and that you are the benchmark! Caveat: Be sure to compare apples to apples. Different libraries collect data different ways. For example, if the process you're benchmarking is checking in and shelving library materials, and Library X checks in and shelves twice as many books an hour as your library does, you might be tempted to adopt their process. However, your library has a particular concern for the condition of your library materials, so your staff sets aside dirty and torn books and other library materials after they've checked them in and cleans and repairs them before shelving them. Library X is not that concerned about the condition of their books. They just keep circulating them until they fall apart. Can you compare your statistics? Not really.

Point 6. Implement the changes to your process (if needed) after answering these questions:

- Do we have the resources to make this change?
- Is it really a better process?
- Will it benefit the public?
- Will it benefit our library economically?
- Will it save staff time?
- Is staff likely to resist this change?
- How disruptive will this change be?
- Will the end result be dramatic enough to make this change worthwhile?

Point 7. If you choose to implement the changes, monitor the results. You may need to modify the process further or even decide to go back to the way you used to do things.

Once a decision has been made, if there is still a lack of consensus, continually promote the positive aspects of the decision, always giving credit to the efforts of the staff. If, for example, the decision has resulted in increased circulation and that has been one of the library's goals, mention that whenever appropriate. If one of the goals has been to increase the number of library users and this decision has resulted in a greater number of users, don't fail to mention it. But don't just *talk* about the change; demonstrate the results and let them speak for themselves. Of course, attitude is everything, so be careful to avoid an in-your-face, I-told-you-so attitude. Always take the high road and remain positive.

While change may be constant, it isn't always instant. Remember that it doesn't happen overnight. Remember three little words: patience, patience, patience!

THE LONG-RANGE PLAN

> By failing to prepare, you are preparing to fail.
> —Benjamin Franklin

How can you achieve your goals and objectives if you don't have any? How can you measure success without a measuring stick? Every library needs a long-range plan.

As the new director, one of the first things you need to do is search for the library's long-range plan. (Ask the secretary! Or the library board.)

Once you've found the plan, make sure you read it immediately. Study it. As much as possible, commit it to memory, or nearly so. If you have not done so before now, have a discussion with the board to make sure that it is the measuring stick that you will be measured against.

While reviewing the plan carefully, study it to see how current it is. Are changes necessary? Where? How soon? Who should make them? What is the procedure in your library for changing the long-range plan?

But what if you discover that the library has no long-range plan? Time to write one! Every library *must* have a plan, just as every well-run business must.

STEPS IN CREATING A LONG-RANGE PLAN

What time period should a long-range plan cover? The experience of many libraries has been that five years is a good time span. Because libraries and technology are changing so quickly, anything longer may be too long. Anything shorter may become too labor intensive because of the amount of effort involved in writing a plan.

Plans generally fall into two types: those that cover a fixed period, and rolling plans. A fixed-period plan would cover a predetermined period, such as 2011–2015. Near the end of that time, you would begin working on a new plan to cover the period 2016–2020.

A rolling plan would also cover a set period, say five years, but each year, the previous year would drop off and another year would be added. For example, the first plan would cover 2007–2011. The next plan would drop 2007 and add 2012, thus covering 2008–2012. The next plan would drop 2008 and add 2013, covering 2009–2013, and so on.

The important thing is that a plan is not static but dynamic. Choose whichever process is workable for *your* library, but choose the process that you *will* follow. Regardless of which type of plan you choose, remember that a plan must be continually updated. Any time circumstances change, the plan will need to be updated.

Step 1: Assemble a Planning Team

With your supervisor, determine who will create the plan. Will library staff create a plan and bring it to the library board or the city or town council for approval? Or will the library board be integrally involved in the process? Or perhaps a special team or committee will be organized to draft the plan.

What are some reasons for using the team approach to planning for your library? An obvious reason is to gather diverse viewpoints. A great deal can be achieved by "groupthink." Also, if the various types of constituencies are represented, it will be easier to get buy-in for your plan once it has been developed and approved. Make sure that your team is representative of your community.

What are some barriers to using the team approach? One of the most obvious, of course, is finding meeting times when everyone can get together. Another is getting people from the various factions to reach consensus. Are there other barriers that you face in your situation? Try to anticipate potential problems and determine beforehand how you will overcome them.

What process will you follow in choosing the team? Perhaps this is predetermined for you by an established procedure or regulation. If not, try to figure out a way to create a team quickly and efficiently.

If you are using the team approach, ask yourself, Who are some of the people you will want on your team? and Who are the stakeholders in your community? You will want to select a broad-based planning team representative of community stakeholders. Included among them:

- Library users
- Local business leaders
- Library staff representing each service area: reference, technical services, children's services, and so forth.
- The library board
- Educators
- Local government officials

Step 2: Prepare the Team

Step two is to prepare the team so that they understand the process of creating a long-range plan and how the library will use the plan. How can you do that? You might want to provide them with some reading matter on the subject. It might be helpful to bring in an outside consultant or facilitator at this point. Or perhaps there is someone on the team or available in your community with this level of business expertise.

Step 3: Perform a Needs Assessment

The long-range planning team should conduct or commission a needs assessment of the library that surveys present services and defines the types of future services that the library might wish to implement. Determine who is qualified to perform this assessment for your library. What qualifications does someone need to conduct such an assessment? Look for someone who's familiar with libraries and how they function. The person should have excellent written and oral communication skills as well as top-notch research abilities. Try to find someone with experience in assessment studies to help with this endeavor. If you need an outside consultant, your state library may be able to give you some leads. Of course, consultants are usually not free, and not even inexpensive, but you might find that the time saved and the quality added to the process make the investment very cost-effective.

What needs to be included in this assessment? It must include a thorough study of your community as well as a thorough study of the library. The difference between what the community wants and needs and what the library currently has to offer is what determines the need. Focus groups made up of community members work well at this point for gathering information.

Step 4: Examine Existing Documents

Review current planning documents; then refine and develop, as needed, a vision statement, a mission statement, and goals for the library. What documents do you have available in your library that would be helpful in creating a long-range plan? Perhaps some evaluation or assessment of the library has been done in the past. Has someone gathered useful statistics? What documents are available in your community outside the library? Are there government documents that might be helpful? Is the annual survey of public libraries in your state by the state library available? If your library doesn't have written goals, a written mission statement, or a written vision statement, it's time to create them.

Check with your organization's planning department to see what's in store for the community surrounding your library over the next few years. The library plan should recognize and complement your city, county, or state master plan.

Mission Statement

The library mission statement is the linchpin of the entire long-range plan. A mission statement is a statement of purpose. It must tell why the library exists. It must answer the question, "What is the purpose of the library?" It is "a summary describing the aims, values, and overall plan of an organization or individual."[1] For instance, the mission statement might be as simple as "To provide an environment where life-long habits of learning, self-improvement and self-expression are encouraged and where patrons can meet their educational, informational and recreational needs."[2]

The key word is "statement." A mission statement is not an essay or a treatise. It should be short enough to remember, if not the exact words, at least the essence.

Vision Statement

A vision statement differs from the mission statement in that it is a declaration of what you want the library to become. As the name implies, it is visionary; it is futuristic. It is a graphic statement of how you see the library at some given point in the future. It is a description of the organization you seek to create.

A good technique for creating a vision statement is simply to relax, close your eyes, and finish the statement, "I see..." What do you envision for the library in the future, perhaps 5 or 10 years from now? What does it look like? What is it doing? What kind of service is it giving? Whom is it serving? What has changed? This can be done as a group exercise, with all members of the team writing down their vision and then sharing ideas with the group.

Step 5: Envision the Plan

Step five takes you toward the future. With the aid of the mission and vision statements and the other data you have gathered, you can start putting together the long-range plan. Determine what services the library currently needs to support and what services you might wish to implement in the future. Are there services that are no longer viable? Are you doing things in which no one has expressed any interest? How do you monitor current and evolving developments in order to gain a vision of future trends? What future services do you envision? What types of resources are needed to support these present and future services? Obviously, this step requires much discussion and group thinking. Blue sky. Dream. Pull out all the stops. Later in the process you can weed out those things that are impractical or too costly.

Step 6: Rank Your Goals

You need to prioritize goals and develop a schedule for implementation. What process will you use to prioritize your goals? What steps do you need to take in developing a schedule for implementation? How long will it take to complete each step?

Step 7: Examine Your Resources

List available and potential resources to support your plan. Which resources are currently available? Which ones are potential resources? What must you do in order to convert those potential resources into available resources? You may have to reallocate resources, which may prove to be a very unpopular move with your staff.

Step 8: Create a Timeline

In order to make sure that things really get done as planned, create a timeline with designations of responsibility. Determine who should perform which task, and develop a realistic timeline for your plan. Be aware of what might affect your schedule, such as staffing levels, vacations, and holidays.

Step 9: Implement the Plan

List the actions that will implement the plan, and then just *do* them!

Step 10: Share the Vision

After the long-range plan has been created (and approved), you will need to share it with the community. Decide who in the community the vision needs to be shared with and the best way to share it with them.

Step 11: Reevaluate

Periodically—at least annually—review, evaluate, and adapt the plan to meet changes in needs. How will you evaluate your progress, formally or informally? Determine how often your plan needs revising. Some libraries do it every year, and some every five years. There's really no magic formula, but if you experience major changes in your community, such as gentrification, rapid growth, or a major influx of diverse cultures, you need to pull out the plan and see if it reflects your "new" community. If it doesn't, it's time for revisions.

IN SUMMARY

It has been said that the only constant is change. While it may not be the only constant, it certainly is an important one. In this day and age, change is certainly inevitable for libraries and librarians, just as in the rest of life. You must be prepared for it.

NOTES

1. Dictionary.com, http://dictionary.reference.com/browse/mission%20 statement. Accessed April 2, 2007.
2. Springfield-Greene County Library District, http://thelibrary.spring field.missouri.org/about/mission.cfm. Accessed February 11, 2007.

GLOSSARY

360 Degree Evaluation. A process involving job-performance feedback from (1) the people supervised by the employee being evaluated, (2) the people who supervise him or her, (3) his or her customers, and (4) his or her peers in the place of employment.

ADA. Americans with Disabilities Act. Legislation that prohibits discrimination against a person on the basis of a disability. It requires that employers make their facilities accessible and provide reasonable accommodation for disabled employees. The text of the act is available at www.ada.gov/pubs/ada.htm.

ADEA. Age Discrimination in Employment Act. Legislation passed in 1967 that prohibits employers from discriminating against employees because of their age. This protected age group starts at age 40. The text of the act is available at www.eeoc.gov/policy/adea.html.

Affirmative Action. A program to combat discrimination against women and minorities. More information is available at www.dol.gov/dol/topic/hiring/affirmativeact.htm#lawregs.

ALA. American Library Association. The national professional organization for librarianship. The Web site for the ALA is www.ala.org.

Alternative Work Schedule. In contrast with an 8-hour, 5-day-a-week work schedule, an alternative schedule consists of, for example, four 10-hour days, nine 9-hour days, and so forth.

Attendance and Leave Policies. Rules that cover bereavement leave, family leave, holidays, jury duty, leaves of absence, maternity leave, military leave, personal leave, sabbaticals, sick leave, and vacations.

At-Will Employment. Employment that has no specified span of duration and can be terminated at any time by the employee or employer for any reason or with no reason stated. "At will" laws vary from state to state.

Benchmarking. A method of measuring your process(es) against the best in the field.

Benefits. Sometimes referred to as "fringe benefits" or "perks" (short for *perquisites*), these are the nonwage "extras" given for working in an organization, such as insurance, tuition reimbursement, car allowances, expense accounts, retirement benefits, and leave time.

Bereavement Leave. Time taken from work due to a death in the family.

BLS. Bureau of Labor Statistics. Part of the Department of Labor, this bureau maintains official statistics on inflation and consumer spending; wages, earnings, and benefits; productivity; safety and health; and so forth. They also produce the *Occupational Outlook Handbook* and the *Monthly Labor Review,* among other publications. The Web site for the BLS is http://stats.bls.gov.

Civil Rights Laws. Legislation that prohibits employers from discriminating against their employees on the basis of race, color, religion, sex, or national origin. The Web page for the Civil Rights Division of the U.S. Department of Justice is www.usdoj.gov/crt.

Classification Plan. A schema showing where everyone in the organization is classified. Sometimes, positions are ranked by points assigned to them for such criteria as education, experience, supervision, decision making (autonomy and impact), contacts, and working conditions. Sometimes, positions are ranked by "broadbanding," which breaks down the organization into such categories as executive, managerial, supervisory, professional, paraprofessional, and clerical bands.

Classification Study. A survey of one or more job classifications that determines where the classification falls in the organizational hierarchy, based on criteria such as education, experience, decision-making authority, working conditions, and supervision.

Coaching. A technique that uses a positive attitude, recognition, and support to encourage employees to do their best.

Collective Bargaining. A process of negotiation between management and union representatives who speak for employees who are union members to determine pay and working conditions.

Compensation. The wages or salary paid for work done.

Consensus. Unanimous agreement among all members of a group.

Cross-training. Having an employee from one department trained to perform duties in another department.

Demotion. Being moved to a lower classification because of a reorganization or disciplinary action.

Disciplinary Action. A corrective measure intended to result in better job performance by the employee being disciplined.

DOL. U.S. Department of Labor. The agency that oversees the compliance of more than 180 labor laws, including those dealing with wages and salaries. The Web page of the DOL is www.dol.gov.

Drug-Free Workplace Act. A federal act passed in 1988 requiring federal contractors or recipients of federal grants to provide a drug-free, alcohol-free workplace. Today, many states, counties, and municipalities have similar standards. The text of the act can be found at http://www.dol.gov/elaws/drugfree.htm.

Dual-Employment Policy. A personnel rule regarding whether or not an employee is allowed to accept outside employment and what types of outside employment are or are not permissible.

EEOC. Equal Employment Opportunity Commission. The EEOC enforces antidiscrimination laws. The Web page of the EEOC is www.eeoc.gov.

Employee Conduct. The way a person acts while on the job.

Employee Grievance Procedure. A process employees can go through if they feel they have been treated badly or unfairly.

Employee Performance Evaluation System. The method used to assess an employee's job performance.

Employee Polygraph Protection Act. Administered by the Wage and Hour Division of the Department of Labor, the Employee Polygraph Protection Act of 1988 bars most employers from using lie detector tests on employees except under certain circumstances. Further information regarding the act and the regulations can be found at www.dol.gov/esa/whd/polygraph.

Employee Recognition. Giving praise, rewards, or awards when an employee's job performance is outstanding.

Empowerment. Giving employees the power to make decisions and act independently. It involves establishing the framework or limits within which the employee may make independent decisions.

EPA. Equal Pay Act. The 1963 federal act mandating equal pay for equal work, regardless of the gender of the employee. The text of the act is available at www.eeoc.gov/policy/epa.html.

Equivalency. When a person applies for a position and doesn't quite meet the minimum qualifications (MQs) as stated in the job announcement or position description, whether in education or experience, this test determines if he or she still qualifies. For example, a person who has more experience than required but not quite as much education might be given an equivalency based on the experience, or vice versa.

ESA. Employment Standards Administration. The mission of the ESA is to "enhance the welfare and protect the rights of American workers." The ESA has four major programs: the Office of Federal Contract Compliance Programs; the Office of Labor-Management Standards; the Office of Workers' Compensation Programs; and the Wage and Hour Division. The ESA Web page is www.dol.gov/esa.

ETA. Employment and Training Administration. The ETA administers federal-government job training, oversees worker-dislocation programs, provides federal grants to the individual states for public-employment service programs, and administers unemployment insurance benefits. Although a federal agency, the ETA provides its services through state and local workforce development systems. The Web page of the ETA is www.doleta.gov.

Exempt Employee. A worker who is exempt from, and not bound by, the Fair Labor Standards Act. Exempt employees are mostly professionals, managers, directors, and so forth, and are paid a salary as opposed to a wage.

External Candidate. An applicant for a position who comes from outside the organization.

FLSA. Fair Labor Standards Act. A federal law that includes the minimum-wage and child-labor laws. Information on the FLSA is available at www.dol.gov/esa/whd/flsa.

FMLA. Family and Medical Leave Act. A federal law that allows employees to take up to 12 weeks of paid or unpaid leave for specific family or medical reasons. Information on the FMLA is available at www.dol.gov/esa/whd/fmla.

Focus Group. A tool for gathering feedback in which a small group of people, representative of a larger constituency, is invited to an open dialogue. Attendees are asked to respond to a set of questions posed by a moderator and usually noted by a recorder.

Garnishment of Wages. Withholding by the employer of part of an employee's wages for certain legally specified reasons.

Golden Rule. "Do to others as you would have them do to you" (Luke 6:31, New International Version).

HIPAA. Health Insurance Portability and Accountability Act. Federal legislation that provides rights for participants and their beneficiaries in group insurance plans. Under this act, exclusion due to pre-existing conditions is limited. Employees and their dependents can't be discriminated against because of the status of their health. Under certain circumstances, HIPAA allows employees to enroll in other plans, purchase individual insurance, or obtain insurance when their benefits run out. Information on HIPAA can be found at www.cms.hhs.gov/HIPAAGenInfo.

Holidays. Time given off work in observance of national holidays. These may include New Year's Eve and New Year's Day, Martin Luther King Day, Presidents' Day, Memorial Day, Fourth of July, Labor Day, Thanksgiving, Christmas Eve, and Christmas. In some areas of the country, Cesar Chavez Day, Columbus Day, Good Friday, Inauguration Day, and others are recognized as holidays. Some organizations give employees what is called a floating holiday, a day they can take off whenever they wish. A list of federal holidays can be found at www.opm.gov/fedhol.

Hostile Work Environment. A condition at the workplace created when there are unwelcome comments or conduct based on sex, race, age, ethnicity, and so forth that interfere with an employee's ability to work or create an intimidating, offensive, or adverse work environment.

Human Resources. Another name for the personnel department of an organization.

Immigration Reform and Control Act. Federal law from 1986 that requires employees to complete a form verifying their identity and authorization to work within three days of beginning their employment. The text of this act can be found at www.oig.lsc.gov/legis/irca86.htm.

Interlibrary Loan. A process for meeting patrons' needs for information by lending resources from one library to another.

Internal Candidate. An applicant for a position who comes from within the organization.

Job Shadowing. A technique that consists of spending time with an employee on the job to see what's involved in his or her duties.

Library Board, Administrative. A body that has the power to hire and fire the director as well as control over the budget.

Library Board, Advisory. A body that makes suggestions and consults with the director. This group has neither control over the budget nor the ability to hire and fire the director.

Limited-Duty Assignment. When an employee is injured, he or she might be put on limited, or light, duty.

MBWA. Managing by Walking Around. A technique for staying in touch with your employees by walking through their work areas, speaking to them, and briefly observing them. This is not to be confused with micromanagement.

Mentoring. A technique of advising, supporting, watching over, and encouraging the progress of a less-experienced person. The process usually involves a longtime employee being assigned to mentor a new employee for a given period of time.

Micromanagement. Paying extreme attention to even the tiniest details, hovering, and watching (and often interfering with) every single thing an employee does.

Military Leave. Taking time off to serve in the military.

Minimum Wage. The federally dictated least amount of money an employer can pay a nonexempt employee for an hour's labor. Current information on the minimum wage can be found at www.dol.gov/dol/topic/wages/minimumwage.htm.

Mission Statement. A formal statement of the purpose of an organization.

Networking. Building and maintaining relationships that are beneficial to your job.

Nonexempt Employee. A worker who is covered under, and not exempt from, the Fair Labor Standards Act. Nonexempt employees are paid hourly wages and receive overtime pay for hours worked above their 40-hour week.

One-on-One Meetings. One person coming together with another person for a discussion.

One-to-One Training. One person teaching another person a skill or set of skills.

Open-Door Philosophy. A combination of: (1) leaving your office door open during work hours and (2) listening to your employees.

OSHA. Occupational Safety and Health Administration. OSHA protects the safety and health of workers; develops and enforces standards; and provides technical assistance, consulting, and training. Much of OSHA's work is done through partnership with the individual states. The Web site for OSHA is www.osha.gov.

Ostrich Management. Sticking one's head in the proverbial sand and ignoring problems, in hopes that they will go away.

Out-of-Class Assignment. An employee performing job duties on a regular basis that are at a higher level than those in his or her job description. Many organizations give assignment pay when this happens. Having employees perform out-of-class assignments in a union environment may create problems with the employee union.

Overtime Pay. Compensation paid to nonexempt employees for hours worked in addition to their normal 40-hour week. Overtime pay is regulated by law.

Personal Leave. Paid or unpaid time taken off for personal business.

Platinum Rule. "Do unto others as they would have you do unto them."

Reasonable Accommodation. Making physical changes to the workplace to enable a person with a disability to work in an organization. It is mandated by law in certain circumstances. Information on reasonable accommodation can be found at www.spb.ca.gov/civilrights/accomodation.htm.

Resignation. This usually refers to voluntary separation from an organization, but involuntary resignation may be part of a disciplinary action.

Retirement. When employees leave a position or career because they have reached an age when they can legally begin to draw retirement benefits.

Retreat. A planning technique involving going somewhere quiet and secluded away from the workplace to plan and reflect on the organization's successes and areas that need improvement.

Sabbatical. A period during which persons temporarily take time off from their job for research or study. These leaves can be either paid or unpaid. Typically, it is a six-month or one-year period taken after seven years in the workplace.

Salary. Regular monetary compensation paid (such as a yearly salary) as opposed to hourly pay.

Selection Process. Screening and interviewing job candidates to select the best person for a particular position.

Separation. An employee leaving a position because of resignation, retirement, workforce reduction, transfer, or other, similar reasons.

Sexual Harassment. Unwanted sexual advances, innuendo, touching, and so forth in the workplace, especially by someone in a position of authority. Sexual harassment is a serious offense and must be treated with zero tolerance.

Sick Leave. Paid time off work due to an employee's illness. In some organizations, employees may use sick leave for the illness of a close family member such as a parent, spouse, or child.

Standby Pay. Compensation for being "on call."

Synergy. The positive effect created by two or more people or things working together in a manner in which the results are greater than the sum of their individual efforts.

Telecommuting. Working off-site but being connected to the workplace through telephone, fax machine, and/or computer.

Title VII. One of the major civil rights bills. The text of Title VII of the Civil Rights Act of 1964 is available at www.eeoc.gov/policy/vii.html.

Turnover Rate. The number of different people in a position over a given period of time or the rate at which the organization gains and loses employees.

USERRA. Uniformed Services Employment and Reemployment Rights Act. A federal act granting certain persons who serve in the armed forces the right to reemployment with their previous employer when they return from service, including those in the Reserves or National Guard. Information about the act can be found at www.osc.gov/userra.htm.

VETS. Veterans' Employment and Training Service. Part of the Department of Labor that provides veterans, Reservists, National Guard, and transitioning service members with the resources and services necessary to succeed in the workforce and protects their employment rights. The Web site for VETS is www.dol.gov/vets.

Wage. Monetary compensation that is paid for each hour worked.

WB. Women's Bureau. Part of the Department of Labor that improves the status of wage-earning women, their working conditions, and their opportunities for advancement. Their Web site is www.dol.gov/wb.

Whistleblower. An employee who reports his or her employer to the authorities for illegal or unethical practices. Information on the Whistleblower Protection Act is available at www.sec.gov/eeoinfo/whistle blowers.htm.

Workforce Reduction. Layoffs, reductions in force (RIFs), and displacements due to reorganization or budgetary cuts.

Workplace Violence. OSHA requires employers to provide each of their employees with a place of employment free from hazards, including violence, that are causing or are likely to cause serious physical harm or even death. OSHA provides information on workplace violence at www.osha.gov/SLTC/workplaceviolence/index.html.

Wrongful Discharge. Termination without cause.

Zero Tolerance. A policy of no exceptions, with immediate disciplinary action taken against an employee because of discriminatory, violent, or sexual behavior.

RESOURCES

MASTER LISTS OF STATE LIBRARY WEB SITES

A number of sites have links to the Web sites of individual state libraries. Because these lists tend to become outdated quickly, we are giving only a few examples:

http://dpi.wi.gov/pld/statelib.html
www.publiclibraries.com/state_library.htm
www.libraryspot.com/libraries/statelibraries.htm
http://lists.webjunction.org/libweb/usa-state.html

INDIVIDUAL STATE LIBRARY WEB SITES

Every state offers some type of support for its libraries, usually, but not always, through the State Library. Often, this support is through a division of the library called something like "Library Development Office." In a few states, the services are administered through the State Department of Education. Below is a list of such agencies followed by the name of the office, department, or service offering support to the public libraries within the state. Web sites change frequently, so you are urged to do your own research if the link appears to be broken.

Alabama	Alabama Public Library Service	http://statelibrary.alabama.gov/Content/Index.aspx
Alaska	Resources & Services for AK Librarians	http://library.state.ak.us/dev/libdev.html
Arizona	Library Development Division	www.dlapr.lib.az.us/extension
Arkansas	Services	www.asl.lib.ar.us/staffser.html
California	Library Development Services (LDS) Bureau	http://www.library.ca.gov/lds/index.html
Colorado	Library Development Services	www.cde.state.co.us/cdelib/LibDev
Connecticut	Division of Library Development	www.cslib.org/dld.htm
Delaware	Delaware's Public Libraries	www.state.lib.de.us/Library_Development/Public_Libraries

Florida	Bureau of Library Development http://dlis.dos.state.fl.us/bld
Georgia	Resources for Libraries www.georgialibraries.org/lib
Hawaii	Hawaii State Public Library System www.librarieshawaii.org
Idaho	Idaho Commission for Libraries http://libraries.idaho.gov/forlibs
Illinois	Library Development Group www.cyberdriveillinois.com/departments/library/who_we_are/development.html
Indiana	Library Development Office (LDO) Division www.statelib.lib.in.us/www/isl/whoweare/ldo.html
Iowa	Library Development www.statelibraryofiowa.org/ld
Kansas	State Library Programs http://skyways.lib.ks.us/KSL/libservices.html
Kentucky	Information/Services for Library Staff www.kdla.ky.gov/libsupport.htm
Louisiana	Library Services http://www.state.lib.la.us/la_dyn_templ.cfm?doc_id=160
Maine	Library Development Division www.statc.me.us/msl/libs
Maryland	Division of Library Development and Services www.marylandpublicschools.org/MSDE/divisions/library
Massachusetts	Advisory Services for Libraries http://mblc.state.ma.us/advisory
Michigan	Library Development and Data Services www.michigan.gov/hal/0,1607,7–160–17451_18668—-,00.html
Minnesota	Library Services and School Technology http://education.state.mn.us/MDE/Learning_Support/Library_Services_and_ School_Technology
Mississippi	Services to Libraries www.mlc.lib.ms.us/ServicesToLibraries/ServicesToLibrariesDefault.htm
Missouri	Library Development www.sos.mo.gov/library/development
Montana	Librarian Services http://msl.state.mt.us/Librarians/Librarians.asp

Nebraska	Nebraska Library Commission www.nlc.state.ne.us
Nevada	Library Planning and Development http://dmla.clan.lib.nv.us/docs/nsla/lpd
New Hampshire	Library Development Services www.nh.gov/nhsl/lds
New Jersey	Library Development Bureau www.njstatelib.org/LDB
New Mexico	Services for New Mexico Libraries www.stlib.state.nm.us/for_libraries_more.php?id=258_0_14_0_M47
New York	Division of Library Development http://www.nysl.nysed.gov/libdev/
North Carolina	Library Development Section http://statelibrary.dcr.state.nc.us/ld/ld.htm
North Dakota	Libraries & Librarians http://ndsl.lib.state.nd.us/Librarian.html
Ohio	Ohio Libraries http://winslo.state.oh.us/publib
Oklahoma	Services to Libraries www.odl.state.ok.us/servlibs
Oregon	Library Development Services www.oregon.gov/OSL/LD
Pennsylvania	Advisory Services for Librarians and Public Library Trustees http://www.statelibrary.state.pa.us/libraries/cwp/view.asp?a=88&Q=38090&librariesNav=|1221|1229||
Rhode Island	Office of Library & Information Services www.olis.state.ri.us
South Carolina	Library Development Division http://www.statelibrary.sc.gov/information-amp-resources-for-librarians.html
South Dakota	Library Development www.sdstatelibrary.com/forlibrarians/development
Tennessee	Planning and Development http://tennessee.gov/tsla/lps/plandev.htm
Texas	Services to Texas Librarians www.tsl.state.tx.us/librarians
Utah	Library Services http://library.utah.gov/library_services

Vermont	Librarians' Resources http://www.libraries.vermont.gov/libraries/library_info.html
Virginia	Library Development & Networking www.lva.lib.va.us/whatwedo/ldnd
Washington	Development of Libraries www.secstate.wa.gov/library/libraries/dev
West Virginia	Programs & Services http://librarycommission.lib.wv.us/libraries.html
Wisconsin	Public Library Development Team http://dpi.wi.gov/pld
Wyoming	Information and Services for Librarians & Information Specialists http://www-wsl.state.wy.us/librarians.html

MASTER LIST OF STATE LIBRARY ASSOCIATIONS

Every state has a state library association. In most cases, there are divisions, chapters, and affiliates. A list of these associations can be found at www.ala.org/ala/ourassociation/chapters/stateandregional/stateregional.htm.

INDIVIDUAL STATE LIBRARY ASSOCIATION WEB SITES

Alabama	Alabama Library Association http://allanet.org
Alaska	Alaska Library Association www.akla.org
Arizona	Arizona Library Association www.azla.org
Arkansas	Arkansas Library Association www.arlib.org
California	California Library Association www.cla-net.org
Colorado	Colorado Association of Libraries www.cal-webs.org
Connecticut	Connecticut Library Association www.ctlibraryassociation.org

Delaware	Delaware Library Association http://www2.lib.udel.edu/dla-crld/index.htm
Florida	Florida Library Association www.flalib.org
Georgia	Georgia Library Association http://gla.georgialibraries.org
Hawaii	Hawaii Library Association http://ohana.chaminade.edu/hla
Idaho	Idaho Library Association www.idaholibraries.org
Illinois	Illinois Library Association www.ila.org
Indiana	Indiana Library Federation www.ilfonline.org
Iowa	Iowa Library Association www.iowalibraryassociation.org
Kansas	Kansas Library Association http://skyways.lib.ks.us/KLA
Kentucky	Kentucky Library Association www.kylibasn.org
Louisiana	Louisiana Library Association www.llaonline.org
Maine	Maine Library Association www.mainelibraries.org
Maryland	Maryland Library Association www.mdlib.org
Massachusetts	Massachusetts Library Association www.masslib.org
Michigan	Michigan Library Association www.mla.lib.mi.us
Minnesota	Minnesota Library Association www.mnlibraryassociation.org
Mississippi	Mississippi Library Association www.misslib.org
Missouri	Missouri Library Association http://molib.org
Montana	Montana Library Association www.mtlib.org

Nebraska	Nebraska Library Association www.nebraskalibraries.org
Nevada	Nevada Library Association www.nevadalibraries.org
New Hampshire	New Hampshire Library Association www.nhlibrarians.org
New Jersey	New Jersey Library Association www.njla.org
New Mexico	New Mexico Library Association www.nmla.org
New York	New York Library Association www.nyla.org
North Carolina	North Carolina Library Association www.nclaonline.org
North Dakota	North Dakota Library Association www.ndla.info
Ohio	Ohio Library Council www.olc.org
Oklahoma	Oklahoma Library Association www.oklibs.org
Oregon	Oregon Library Association www.olaweb.org
Pennsylvania	Pennsylvania Library Association www.palibraries.org
Rhode Island	Rhode Island Library Association www.uri.edu/library/rila
South Carolina	South Carolina Library Association www.scla.org
South Dakota	South Dakota Library Association www.sdlibraryassociation.org
Tennessee	Tennessee Library Association www.tnla.org
Texas	Texas Library Association www.txla.org
Utah	Utah Library Association www.ula.org
Vermont	Vermont Library Association www.vermontlibraries.org

Virginia	Virginia Library Association www.vla.org
Washington	Washington Library Association www.wla.org
West Virginia	West Virginia Library Association www.wvla.org
Wisconsin	Wisconsin Library Association www.wla.lib.wi.us
Wyoming	Wyoming Library Association www.wyla.org

NATIONAL ASSOCIATIONS

American Library Association   www.ala.org
Public Library Association   www.pla.org

REGIONAL ASSOCIATIONS

New England Library Association   www.nelib.org
Mountain Plains Library Association   www.mpla.us
Pacific Northwest Library Association   www.pnla.org
Southeastern Library Association   http://sela.jsu.edu

INDEX

ABOUT THE AUTHORS

DENNIS C. TUCKER began his library career as a school librarian in the Missouri Bootheel. From there, he became director of the library at Bethel College in Mishawaka, Indiana, and worked at several other libraries in the area, including the Mishawaka Public Library. He spent more than a decade in several positions at Indiana Cooperative Library Services (INCOLSA). Tiring of winter, he moved to Natchitoches, Louisiana, to become Director of Libraries at Northwestern State University. Next came sunny California, where he served as Director of Learning Resources at Modesto Junior College and now works as a library consultant for his own company, Tucker and Associates. Author of numerous books and articles, his monographs include *Pathways to Nursing: A Guide to Library and Online Research in Nursing and Allied Health* (2004), *Research Techniques for Scholars and Students in Religion and Theology* (2000), and *Library Relocations and Collection Shifts* (1999). He served as contributing editor on *Basic Information Technology Skills* (2002). Tucker has been very involved professionally and has served as president of the Louisiana chapter of the Association of College and Research Libraries (ACRL), and as chair of the Library and Information Technology Association (LITA) International Relations Committee. He has been actively involved with the International Relations Round Table (IRRT) of the American Library Association. A frequent presenter of workshops and conferences, he has spoken across the United States as well as in Europe and Central and South America. Before entering the field of library and information science, he served many years as a foreign-language teacher, and a long time before that, he was an award-winning tour guide. Tucker holds a Ph.D. from Foundation House/Oxford, an MLS from the University of Missouri, and an MAT from Southeast Missouri State University.

SHELLEY ELIZABETH MOSLEY began her library career as a school librarian, and then moved to the Glendale Public Library in Arizona. After 3 years as a reference librarian, she became the library's technical services manager. Mosley then became the manager of the Velma Teague Branch Library and remained in that position for 18 years. She received two Arizona Society for Public Administration awards—one for Arizona Supervisor of the Year and one she shared as head of the city's benchmarking team for the Arizona Work Team of the Year. Mosley has been a member of more than 150 job-interview teams and has facilitated long-range plans for other Arizona libraries. A member of Beta Phi Mu, the international library honor society, Mosley spends her so-called retirement as a full-time writer, reviewer, and adjunct librarian at Glendale Community College. She has been a contributor to the reference series What Do I Read Next? since 1999 and has coauthored several nonfiction books, including *The Suffragists in Literature for Youth: The Fight for the Vote; Romance Today: An A-to-Z Guide to Contemporary American Romance Writers;* and *The Complete Idiot's Guide to the Ultimate Reading List.* Her writings include articles in *Library Journal, Booklist, VOYA,* and the *Wilson Library Bulletin,* two of which were awarded the Romance Writers of America's Veritas Award for journalistic excellence. In addition to being named the Romance Writers of America's Librarian of the Year, Mosley has coauthored five romantic comedies and one novella under the pseudonym Deborah Shelley (www.deborahshelley.com).